MW01127467

Poetic Scripture

Genesis to Ruth Stories of the Bible in Poetic Form

LaMar Smith

WESTBOW
PRESS®
A DIVISION OF THOMAS NELSON
& ZONDERVAN

Copyright © 2017 LaMar Smith.

All rights reserved. No part of this book may be used or reproduced by any means, graphic, electronic, or mechanical, including photocopying, recording, taping or by any information storage retrieval system without the written permission of the author except in the case of brief quotations embodied in critical articles and reviews.

This book is a work of non-fiction. Unless otherwise noted, the author and the publisher make no explicit guarantees as to the accuracy of the information contained in this book and in some cases, names of people and places have been altered to protect their privacy.

Scripture taken from the King James Version of the Bible.

WestBow Press books may be ordered through booksellers or by contacting:

WestBow Press
A Division of Thomas Nelson & Zondervan
1663 Liberty Drive
Bloomington, IN 47403
www.westbowpress.com
1 (866) 928-1240

Because of the dynamic nature of the Internet, any web addresses or links contained in this book may have changed since publication and may no longer be valid. The views expressed in this work are solely those of the author and do not necessarily reflect the views of the publisher, and the publisher hereby disclaims any responsibility for them.

Any people depicted in stock imagery provided by Thinkstock are models, and such images are being used for illustrative purposes only. Certain stock imagery © Thinkstock.

ISBN: 978-1-9736-1017-5 (sc)
ISBN: 978-1-9736-1016-8 (hc)
ISBN: 978-1-9736-1018-2 (e)

Library of Congress Control Number: 2017918681

Print information available on the last page.

WestBow Press rev. date: 12/15/2017

Contents

Special Thanks.. xi

Introduction... xiii

Thank You.. xv

Genesis

The Beginning 1

The Garden 2

Brother's Keeper 4

The Ark 6

Abram to Abraham 8

Salt and Influence 13

Two Sons, Two Journeys... 15

Test of Faith.. 17

War in the Womb 19

Brother's Deceit 21

Birth of the Twelve... 23

Deception to Forgiveness... 24

Baby Sister's Eleven... 26

Dream to Nightmare 28

Duty Bound.. 30

When the Cat's Away... 32

Prisoner to Prince.. 34

Feast and Famine 36

Silver Lining 38

Pharaoh's Wealth... 40

Blessings and Death...41

Dear Father

Family/Friends 47

Love 48

Gifts 49

Mercy 50

Forgive 51

Alone 52

Unworthy 53

When I'm Weak 54

My Job 55

Dear Lord 56

The Lord's Answer 57

Thanks 58

A Prayer for Freedom 59

Exodus

River of Death and Life 63

Prophecy 65

I Am 67

Displeasure near Death 69

Busin Bricks 71

Diamond Hard 73

Song of Deliverance 78

The Fear of God 80

Exodus 20—The Ten 82

Guardian Angel 84

History Lesson 86

Stiff Neck 88

Poems

My Oath 93

First Stone 94

His Place 95

Lighted Path 96

Legal Issues 97

In God We Trust 98

Spin It (To Positivity) 99

Heaven and Hell 100

Leviticus

I Am Holy 104

Haikus

Peace/Joy 109

War/Lost 109

Near/Now 109

Love/Divine 109

Day/Pray 109

Blood/Grace 110

Death/Love 110

March 110

Stand Up 110

True 110

Selfless 110

One or Two 111

First/Last 111

Down 111

Foundation 111

Point 111

Signs 111

Path 112

Two 112

Sing 112

Waters 112

Time 112

Numbers

Curse of the Womb 117

Ask and Receive 119

Simply Put 121

My Choice 123

Staff and Duty 125

Rock of Disobedience 127

Sight and Voice 129

Backfire 131

Seduction and Destruction 133

Poems

Shhh (God's Silence)...137

Mighty Is It...139

Two Commandments 141

He's Coming..143

NCE, ESS, and ISS 145

Flesh..146

Deuteronomy

King 149

Purge 150

Poems

Joy in Heaven..155

Consumption..156

Mother's Prayer...158

Tithing...159

Joshua

Twelve Stones and a Prostitute.. 164

Trader and a Spear 167

Thirty-One Flavors 169

Satan, the Devil, Lucifer

I'm a Bad Man 176

He Made Me Do It 179

Nuthin' on Him..182

True Faith..184

Judges

A Judge, a Peg, and a Woman... 190

A Fleece and the Three Hundred Birth of a Hero—Part I 192

A Fleece and the Three Hundred Death of Gideon—Part II...............195

Millstone Judge...198

Hasty Vow 200

Biblical Superman...202

The Three Hundred Tails of Superman 205

Superman's Kryptonite 207

Pieces of Twelve 209

Concubine's War 211

Poems

Son's Pride 217

Mom the Matriarch 218

Open Heart... 220

Days of the Week 221

Blessed 222

High-Low 223

Here I Stand 224

Ruth

Call Me Mara 230

Grains of Redemption.. 232

Famous Bloodline 234

Closing

Special Thanks

First and foremost, I must thank the Father of the universe. Our dear kind and loving God and Savior. He is absolutely the reason for my gift of poetry and writing this book. Thank you for your forgiveness and your love. I know at times I am so underserving and that I may be in the future. You have forgiven me at my lowest and at my highest. I am grateful, humble, and thankful for your mercy and grace. Nothing we do is without your blessing. All we have we owe to you; all of this belongs to you. As I strive to be a better Christian in your eyes, allow me to keep you close in my heart, mind, body, and soul. Let your will be done.

A special thanks to my family and friends. All had a part in my spiritual growth in one form or another, and I am grateful for the experience. My mom, a true inspiration in my life and the lives of others. Keep striving to the kingdom. My many brothers and close friends that are: Wendell Allmon, Derek Sharpe, Ron Davids, James Peteet, Pat Baker, Mike McCadney, and Teddy Taylor.

To my sisters: Shawn Hill, Jennifer Roan, and to my lady Melody Y. Hill. My extended family of aunts, uncles, cousins, nieces, and nephews (big Josh). I cannot forget the pastors that speak the truth about the Father; your sermons were and are much appreciated. Thank you to the reader for taking the time to read my poetry. I hope it blesses you to stay on the path to Jesus and eternal life. He is the only answer to our prayers. The more you open your heart to Him, the more He will bless you. There is only one true God, and He is a jealous God. Place God first in your life above all else. Pray for me and my shortcomings, as I will pray for you.

One love.

Amen.

Introduction

My never-ending theme is to give God all the glory because with Him all is possible. He's given me the ability to write poetry, and I am giving back the gift to anyone I can. All is possible through Christ, and through Him we can achieve anything. He is the only answer to all our problems; all we have to do is ask.

This book is a poetic summary of biblical stories from Genesis to Ruth. When you read, you will understand I have not taken away the message the Father has given us in His holy Word. This is another tool to be used to spread His message to others, to be fishers of men with the gift God has given. After all, that is what we should do. Help others find Jesus; help others in their journey to God. I hope this book does that for you.

You will find between each book of the Bible different styles of poems, but all reflect upon a journey to Christ. These pieces have a personal touch with my journey, my spin, my feelings and emotions. The Bible I used as a reference was the King James Version, but if you enjoy reading a different translation, then do so. The mission is to have you read God's words in a translation you enjoy reading. As long as you read four pages per day, you can read His words in one year. Our heavenly Father is amazing. He wants the best for all of us. He wants us to go to heaven with Him when He comes again. Love Him, obey Him, honor Him, praise Him, and watch the blessing pour in. Bless you all.

Amen.

Thank You

I want to thank you for giving life to me.

That's why I'm giving praises down on bended knees.

Thank you for the unconditional love you give to me,

Even when I acted a fool and didn't believe.

Thank you for giving your Son's life for me.

That's why I'm singing praises and giving this testimony.

Testimony of your magnificent power and wonderful love,

Testimony of the one true God above.

Thank you for the food I am able to eat.

Thank you for the words I formulate when I speak.

Thank you for waking me every morning when you don't have to,

For letting me rest, gaining my strength and making it anew.

Thank you for allowing me to solve problems with my mind.

Thank you for your insight and for not being blind,

Blind to your beauty and your glorious wisdom,

And keeping me focused in prayer to see your kingdom.

There is so much I can thank my God for.

That's why I will love Him forever more.

Amen.

Before you start to read the following poems, I suggest you pick up a Bible that you can understand. There are many different translations to choose from. Please get one that you can understand and look up the reference verses at the end of most of the poems, which are a good focal point to completely read the story. This is my way of thanking God for the talent He has given me. Whether you agree with my poems are not, hopefully you will read the Bible for yourself and enjoy God's words.

A good friend who is actually like a brother to me, Pastor Derek Sharp, told me you can read the Bible from Genesis to Revelation in one year without straining yourself. Divide the number of pages in the Bible by the 365 days in a year. It's about four pages a day. Surely we read e-mails and social media in excess of four pages. Can we not give our creator four pages a day? God does not ask for much from us if we really think about it: the faith of a mustard seed, 10 percent of our earnings, love your neighbor and love God. There is more to it than that, but I think you get the meaning. This can sometimes be difficult to do, and I am just as guilty of noncompliance as most of you. I can say the journey to become closer to my heavenly Father is a wonderful journey. My journey has been filled with my share of heartaches, setbacks, turmoil, and tears. But the reward in the end outweighs anything that this earth can give. The possibility of meeting the Father of heaven and earth. Can you imagine that! Everlasting life with God! If anyone can describe that, I would love to hear it.

Genesis

The Beginning

When there was a void and nothing in space,
God created the earth and put it in its place.
And with the power of His might,
He said, "Let there be light."
On the second day, this is the action of the Most High.
He separated the waters and called the space the sky.
What did He do on day three?
He made the plants and fruit with seeds.
Also what He did on day three,
He separated dry land from the seas.
On day four, with all this in His sight,
He made the sun for day and the moon for night.
What did He do on day five?
He made the fish of the sea and the birds that fly.
On day six, He made all creatures and all animals.
The ones that crawled, reptiles, livestock, and the mammals.
On day six, with almost everything complete,
He called the man Adam, and Adam named Eve.
With all the universe looking in awe, God stood.
And He saw what He did and said, "This is good."
With all that was good, this is what happened on day seven.
He blessed everything and rested in heaven.

How great God is to create all life in just six days. All animals and insects have a specific purpose on this Earth to continue the circle of life that God created. Think about this: one animal eats an insect; another eats that animal, and insects eat the remains; then it is recycled into the earth, which repeats the circle of life. The plants on earth are essential for the air we breathe and food for all life, but each plant serves a purpose. Do you think you could create a planet and have every plant, animal, air, water, sun, and sky all serving a specific purpose to function in harmony?

God is amazing!

(Gen. 1:3–5, Gen. 1:6–9, Gen. 1:11–13, Gen. 1:14–19, Gen. 1:20–23, Gen. 1:24–31, Gen. 2:1–3)

The Garden

The serpent told Eve just to take a bite.

"If you do, you and God will be just alike.

Your eyes will be open, and you'll have insight.

You will know the difference between wrong and right."

Eve did eat the fruit, and it was pleasing to the eyes.

The desire was there to make her smart and wise.

Only until Adam ate the fruit, which started the curse.

This only happened because God had made Adam first.

In the garden, God called out for Adam and Eve.

But they were ashamed and hid themselves with fig leaves.

God asked Adam, "Why did you eat from the knowledge tree?"

"I didn't; it was given to me by my wife, Eve."

Eve said, "The serpent words were truth mixed with lies.

After I ate the fruit, I didn't surely die."

Now they knew they were naked and they were bare.

Because of disobedience, their shame they had to share.

God said, "Serpent, didn't you know these children are mine?

Therefore, I curse you to crawl on your belly for all time.

Serpent, I curse you because you let Satan in,

Because when I made you, you were void of sin.

To Eve, I will sharpen the pain during the time you give birth.

To Adam, to eat, you will have a hard time working the earth.

To Satan, there will be fighting between your seed and her seed.

You shall bruise his heel, and your head, he shall bruise thee."

God banished Adam to keep him from the life tree.

God said, "If he eats the fruit, he'll have the power of immortality."

God said, "If Adam eats from the tree, he'll become like us.

So from the ground you were made, ye shall return to the dust."

During this time, the serpent did not always crawl on its belly. Could the serpent fly? Or walk? But we do know it was craftier than any other creature the Lord made. Think about this: Could the other animals talk or just the serpent? Was it because Satan entered the serpent, which allowed it to speak?

If Eve had believed more in God than a deceptive serpent, sin would never have entered in our minds and hearts. Adam and Eve spoke with the Lord daily about anything on their minds. Can you imagine a better teacher than God? We need to remember that Adam and Eve did not have a childhood; they were created as adults. Therefore, their minds were as children because they didn't get daily life lessons that a mother and father would give a child. The same lesson from creation still reigns supreme today: trust God first and only!

(Gen. 3:4–5, Gen. 3:6–8, Gen. 9:9–11, Gen. 3:11–15, Gen. 3:14–15, Gen. 3:16–19, Gen. 3:24, Gen. 3:22)

Brother's Keeper

Cain and Abel, you two are the first of brothers.

You share a bond greater than any others.

God showed favor of Abel's offering but not that of Cain's.

Because of this, Cain became jealous, and it drove him insane.

Cain took Abel in the field, and Cain committed the first homicide.

Never again will Cain have his brother, Abel, by his side.

God asked Cain, "Where is your brother? For it is he whom I seek."

Cain said, "I don't know. Is it up to me, my brother I should keep?"

God knew Cain's words were false and his words were untrue.

Then God asked, "Cain, my son, what did you do?

Because your offering did not please me!

You killed your brother, Abel, out of jealousy!

Your brother, Abel, is gone, and he cannot be found,

But his lifeblood cries out to me from the ground.

And because of sin and fear, you lied to me.

Now I have no choice but to place a mark on thee.

Seven times greater vengeance if anyone kills you with their hands.

You will be hidden from my presence and driven from these lands.

When you work the land, no crops will harvest for you,

No matter how hard you work and no matter what you do.

Cain, I still love you because I am your God,

But leave my presence and go live in the land of Nod.

Sin is crouching at your door but over it; you have the power.

Do what is right. If not, the sin in you will self-devour."

The first two brothers on the planet, and one was jealous of the other. We would love to believe the first would have an unbreakable bond. There isn't any mention of Satan directly, but do you think because of their parents' sin, it was inherited by the children? We now know sin tore the first family apart with lies, deception, and eventually murder.

This is a powerful story about what not to do with your siblings. Don't succumb to jealousy, anger, or hatred, not only with your siblings but with anyone. Have you ever heard this: "I wish you were more like your brother or sister"? How did that make you feel? Hopefully not feelings of wanting to harm them, but at the same time, it makes you feel less than a person. Less than you. God showed us how to show mercy and forgiveness because He could have struck Cain down, but that wouldn't bring Abel back. Can we enter the kingdom without forgiveness?

(Gen. 4:1–2, Gen. 4:3–5, Gen. 4:8, Gen. 4:9–11, Gen. 4:15, Gen. 4:12, Gen. 4:16, Gen. 4:7)

The Ark

During Noah's time, there was no such thing as rain.

Water came from the earth because it was self-sustained.

The earth was watered from within through the ground.

The wickedness of humankind forced God to bring the rain down.

The giants of the earth did anything that they pleased,

But God heart was hurt, and His heart grieved.

Anything that humankind could imagine, humankind did.

With a heavy heart, God said, "How can I let humans live?"

God said, "My Spirit shall not always strive with humans.

Because they are flesh, they will have 120-year life span.

All shall perish; I will wipe them from this place.

Only Noah, in my eyes, has found my mercy and grace.

Make an ark because all my creatures shall die.

I will make a covenant with you and give you life,

All creatures that crawl, fly, and all that creep,

Two of every kind and all manner of beasts.

All shall come to enter my ark of salvation.

Noah and thy house, I have seen a righteous generation.

For when the rain comes for forty days and forty nights,

I will destroy all I have made. I will destroy all life."

God sealed the ark when Noah and his family were within.

God had to destroy all because of humankind's sin.

After 150 days, a dove and raven were released.

Noah did this to find out if the waters receded.

In another seven days, the dove returned with a fresh olive leaf.

It was almost time for all the animals to be released.

The second time the dove was released, it continued to fly.

This is when Noah knew that the ground was almost dry.

God said, "Release all that creep and all that fly.

Go forth, be fruitful, and multiply.

My covenant will be the rainbow in the sky,

A symbol that never again will I destroy all life."

How wicked humankind must have been for God to decide that human life must end. Could you destroy your own children? On the other hand, could you decide which one of your children should live and which must die? What a decision and heavy grief must have been in God's heart.

The ark itself must have been huge to house a pair of all life inside its hull. Think about the task of cleaning and feeding of all these creatures. And the smell. But when you are on a mission from God and with God, nothing is too great. The rainbow in the sky is God's word that he will not destroy life by water ever again. God is constant and does not break his word.

(Gen. 6:5–7, Gen. 2:6, Gen. 7:4, Gen. 6:3, Gen. 6:8–19, Gen. 8:6–12, Gen. 9:12–17)

Abram to Abraham

This is the story of a man named Abram.

Through his faith, God changed his name to Abraham.

The Lord said, "Go from this country to a land I will show you.

I will make you a great nation, and abundantly I will bless you.

You will be a blessing to all, and your name will be great.

Those who bless you or curse you, I will give them the same fate,

And all the people on Earth will be blessed through you."

So Abram went from the land as the Lord told him to do.

He took his nephew Lot, wife, Sarai, and set out for Canaan lands.

Eventually after some time, they entered into the Egyptian sands.

Abram told Sarai, "Tell the Egyptians you are my sister, not my wife.

You are beautiful; they will let you live but take my life."

It was so. Pharaoh took her, and Abram acquired cattle, servants, and sheep.

Because of Sarai, the Lord inflicted on Pharaoh and household serious disease.

Pharaoh summoned Abram and asked, "What have you done to me?

This is your wife, not your sister. Now take her and leave."

Abram and Sarai left with everything they had, as they were told.

After time passed, Abram became wealthy in livestock, silver, and gold.

Abram's nephew Lot with his herds was still traveling by his side,

But their combined herds were numerous; the land they had to divide.

Neither wanted quarreling to divide the family.

Abram said, "If you go west, I will go east."

Lot chose east to live in the Jordan plain,

Close to Sodom were people sinned against the Lord's name.

After Lot parted, the Lord said to Abram, "Look around where you are.

I give you this land, and make your descendants as numerous as the stars."

In time, the nine kings of the lands went to war.

Some men fled, and some fell in the pits of tar.

Lot and his family were taken during this conflict.

Abram called 318 trained men to free Lot as a captive.

North of Damascus, Abram divided his men and attacked at night.

He recovered all the goods, possessions and saved his nephew's life.

Abram returned home after the allied kings were defeated.

The king of Sodom came out to meet him in the Shaveh Valley.

Then bread and wine was brought out by the Salem's king.

He blessed Abram, and Abram gave him a tenth of everything.

The king of Sodom said, "Keep all the goods and give the people to me."

But Abram said, "I swore an oath. I will take nothing. I have all I need

You will not be able to say, 'I have made Abram wealthy.'

I take only the share that belongs to the men that went with me."

Later, in a vision to Abram, came the Word of the Lord.

The Lord said, "I am your shield, your very great reward."

But Abram said, "I have no heir or sons that can carry on my seed."

God said, "Look in the sky and count the stars; so shall your offspring be.

I brought you out of Ur of the Chaldeans to give you these lands.

I am giving it to you as your possession by my own two hands."

"How do I know that I will gain possession of it?" Abram asked.

God said, "Bring me a heifer, a goat, and ram and cut them in half,

Each three years of age, along with a young pigeon and dove.

Offer them as a sacrifice to the one true God above."

At sunset, a thick and dreadful darkness fell on Abram as he went to sleep.

God said, "You will be buried at a good old age, going to your ancestors in peace.

However, four hundred years your descendants will be enslaved in a foreign country.

Afterward, they will come out with great possessions, my covenant to thee."

Now Sarai, Abram's wife, had not been blessed to conceive.

She gave Abram her slave Hagar as a wife to start a family.

When Hagar became pregnant, she began to despise her mistress.

Sarai said to Abram, "You are the cause for my suffering and stress.

I put my slave in your arms, now she hates me.

May the Lord judge between you and me."

Abram said, "Your slave is in your hands."

She mistreated Hagar, so Hagar fled from the lands.

The angel of the Lord found Hagar in the desert by the spring.

He said, "Hagar, slave of Sarai, where are you from and where are you going?"

She answered, "From my mistress, Sarai, I am running away."

He said, "Go back and submit to her. Do not dismay,

For the Lord has heard of your misery,

And your descendants I will increase.

Your son will be a wild man like an untamed donkey.

All hands will be against him. He will live in hostility."

The first of Abram's children, bore by Hagar, the Egyptian slave.

She gave birth to a son, and Ishmael was the name she gave.

Abram was eighty-six with his first child. Now Abram was ninety-nine.

God said, "Walk before me faithfully, and I will bless you for all time.

Then I will make my covenant between you and me.

I will bless you and increase your numbers greatly."

Abram fell facedown before the Lord of all creations.

God said, "Abram, you will be the father of many nations.

I will make you very fruitful, and kings will come from you.

I will establish my covenant and to your descendants after you.

No longer will you be called Abram; your name is now Abraham.

I am giving to your possession this whole land of Canaan.

Keep my covenant, you and your descendants for generations to come.

Every male among you shall be circumcised from old to young,

An everlasting covenant in your flesh.

Those uncircumcised will be cut off from the rest.

As for your wife, Sarai, Sarah so shall her name be.

I will give you a son by her and bless her abundantly."

Abraham laughed and said to himself, "We are both too old to have kids.

If only Ishmael will fall under your blessings that he may live."

"Isaac is the name when Sarah bears you a son,

And Ishmael will be the father of twelve rulers when I'm done."

Abraham was ninety-nine years old, and Ishmael was a teenager.

Circumcision took place for all, including those bought by a foreigner.

At Mamre, the Lord appeared to Abraham while he was near the great trees.

Three men standing nearby, he hurried from his tent to go out and greet.

They sat, ate, and washed their feet.

Abraham stood near them under a tree.

One said, "This time next year, you will have a son by Sarah, your wife."

Sarah laughed and said, "I am too worn out to enjoy my child's life."

Then the Lord said to Abraham, "Why did Sarah laugh?

Is there anything too hard for the Lord to come to pass?"

The men looked toward Sodom when they got up to leave.

The Lord said, "Shall I hide my will from Abraham so he won't grieve?

I have blessed him.

I have chosen him.

The outcry against Sodom and Gomorrah is so grievous and so great.

I will go to see if it's true. If so, they have sealed their own fate."

The men turned away and went toward Sodom, but Abraham remained.

Abraham said, "Will you sweep away the righteous and wicked just the same"

What if there are fifty righteous people in the city?

Will you spare them and show them pity?"

The Lord said, "If I find fifty people, I will spare it for their sake."

Abraham said, "My Lord, if there are five less, will it be the same fate?"

The Lord said, "If I find forty-five, I will not destroy it."

Abraham asked, "And if forty are found, will you spare it?"

The Lord said, "I will not destroy it for the sake of forty."

Abraham said, "Please don't be angry, but let me speak.

What if only thirty righteous people can be found there?"

The Lord answered, "For the sake of the thirty, the city will be spared."

Abraham said, "I have been bold to speak. What if twenty can be found?"

The Lord said, "I will spare it because I am honor bound."

"Please spare them for ten." Abraham spoke one last time.

The Lord said, "I will not destroy it for ten, if ten I can find."

The Lord finished speaking with Abraham, and Abraham went home.

The three angels went to Sodom and destroyed the city made of brick and stone.

Abraham arose the next morning and stood in the same place.

Smoke rising from the land like a furnace, he knew Sodom's fate.

Toward the lands of the plain, the smoke was dense.

Here is Lot's journey as you read "Salt and Influence"

(Gen. 12–18, Gen. 19:27–29)

After reading some of Abraham's story, are you not convinced that God can do anything? What a God we serve! The journey He placed Abraham on had war, abduction, and children, only to be rewarded for faith. All of this was done at an age when most of us are ready to retire. How about God informing Abraham that kings would come from his bloodline. Do you think Abraham knew which king? Do we know who our bloodline will produce? The point is to keep serving God faithfully and let Him do exactly what He does. Abraham's journey is not over, and we will continue after the story of Lot. Remember, four pages per day and a Bible translation that you understand. Enjoy God's Word and keep reading. As a hint, keep in mind when Abram told Sarai to inform anyone that asked, they are brother and sister.

Salt and Influence

God will rain down fire and burning sulfur from the sky.

The Lord sent us to destroy all because He heard the sinful outcry.

The angels knew that Abraham pleaded for his people.

Because of him, Lot will be spared from all this evil.

"You don't want to see God's wrath when destruction begins.

Even when Abraham pleaded for the righteous from fifty down to ten.

Take your family and hurry to leave the city.

My wrath will be swift, for I will have no pity."

"Let them out" were the words of the angry mob.

They wanted to have sex with strangers sent by God.

Lot said, "Leave the strangers alone and let them be.

I will send out my daughters. Do with them as you please."

The evil in their hearts caused God to strike them blind.

They grew weary of the door they could not find.

The angels asked if there were other relatives in this place.

"Gather them quickly. Do not delay and do not haste."

The angels rushed Lot's family out because of his hesitation.

"We will destroy this city and others, including all life and vegetation."

Lot was told to take his family and not to look back.

His wife was turned to salt because of the faith she lacked.

After escape, Lot's daughters got him drunk with wine.

They had sex with their father to continue their bloodline.

The older first, who gave birth to the Moabites.

Then the younger, who started the line of the Ammonites.

The influence of Sodom's evil was evident in Lot's life,

The incest of his daughters, and it destroyed Lot's wife.

When God destroyed Sodom and Gomorrah, this wasn't the only city on His list of destruction (Gen. 19:25). Does this famous city sound familiar to our cities of today? Are our cities any different from Sodom and Gomorrah? Could we find enough righteous people in our city to keep God from destroying it?

As a person always around evil, one would think eventually some sin will influence our lives. Is this what happened to Lot? The evil around him had a major influence on his entire family. What kind of hold does evil have on you? How much influence do others have on your life to have you to do wrong? God knows evil is all around us, but He doesn't want us to be consumed or influenced to the point we turn from Him. Pray for strength and run from evil and let your faith influence others.

(Gen. 18:20–21, Gen. 18:24–32, Gen. 19:5, Gen. 19:8, Gen. 19:11, Gen. 19:16–17, Gen. 19:25–26, Gen. 19:31–38)

Two Sons, Two Journeys

After Sodom was destroyed, the land was charred and in disarray.

Abraham moved into the Negev region, and Gerar is where he stayed.

Abraham said, about Sarah, "She is my sister," to everyone that lived there.

King Abimelech took Sarah for himself, thinking they're not a married pair.

God said to Abimelech in a dream, "You are dead because of the woman you've taken."

Abimelech had not gone near her and said, "You will destroy an innocent nation.

I have done this with a clear conscience and with clean hands."

She said, "He is my brother. I didn't know she was married to the man."

God said, "I know. That is why I didn't allow you to touch his wife.

But if you don't return her, you and all belonging to you will die.

He is a prophet, and for you he will pray."

Summoning his officials, he told them, and they were afraid.

Then Abimelech called Abraham and said, "What have you done"

How have I wronged you, to bring great guilt on my kingdom?"

"There is no fear of God in this place," Abraham replied.

"I had to say Sarah is my sister; if not, they would take my life.

Besides she really is my sister, the daughter of my father's household.

I said to her, 'Show your love to me by saying that everywhere we go.'"

Abimelech gave Abraham flock, slaves, and said, "My land is before you,

Sarah is vindicated, a thousand pieces of silver to cover the offense against you."

Abraham prayed to God, and God healed Abimelech's entire family.

Again all females in Abimelech's household were able to conceive.

God did this because Sarah had not conceived up to this day.

Soon God kept His promise, and Sarah gave birth in her old age.

Isaac was born, and Abraham was one hundred years old.

God did all as promised, which is what Abraham was told.

Now with two sons, this strengthened Abraham's belief,

Both of them with different paths and different journeys.

When Isaac grew, he was weaned, and Abraham had a great feast.

But Sarah said, "Get that slave woman and her son away from me.

They will never share in my son's inheritance."

Ishmael was also Abraham's son, and he was stressed.

But God said, "Listen to Sarah, your wife, about your slave and your son,
Because it is through your son Isaac that your offspring will be reckoned.
I will make the son of the slave a nation because he is your offspring."
Abraham gave them food and water and sent them away in the morning.
In the Desert of Beersheba, they wandered, and their water was gone.
She placed Ishmael under a bush, and without water it wouldn't be long.
"I cannot watch the boy die."
God said, "I have heard his cry."
An angel from heaven said, "Don't fear. Lift him and take him by the hand.
I will make him into a great nation, the father of many rulers across the land."
She saw a well of water when God opened her eyes.
She filled the skin with water, which saved their lives
Ishmael grew, became an archer, and the desert is where he lived.
Hagar got him a wife from Egypt, and God fulfilled His promise.

Now we know Sarah was Abraham sister on his father's side. God keeps His promise. No matter what adversities we go through, once God says something, it is done. Did Abraham's faith waver? Should yours? With all we go through, our faith needs to be just as strong as Abraham's. Again, is there anything God can't do? Pregnancy at their age? And healthy. What a God. In this story, Abraham had to send his firstborn away in the desert. Could you do that? Sending his son into the unknown based on faith could not have been easy. If you think Abraham's faith was strong, keep reading what he had to do in "Test of Faith."

(Gen. 17:20, Gen. 20 and 21)

Test of Faith

"Abraham."

"Here I am."

God said, "Take your son, your only son whom you love,

And sacrifice him to me, the one true God above.

Sacrifice him as a burnt offering on a mountain I will show you.

Take Isaac to the region of Moriah, and there you know what to do."

The next morning, Abraham took two servants, his son, and loaded his donkey.

He cut enough wood for the burnt offering he needed to complete.

On the third day, Abraham looked up and saw the place in the distance.

He said to his servants, "Stay here with the donkey because this is it.

After I and the boy go to worship, we will come back to you."

Abraham did not say one word about the task he had to do.

He placed the wood on Isaac, and he carried the fire and the knife,

The same knife that would soon take his son Isaac's life.

"Father?" asked Isaac, his son.

Abraham replied, "Yes, my son."

"We have fire and wood but no lamb in the place we need to reach."

Abraham replied, "God himself will provide the burnt offering we seek."

Abraham built an altar, and on top of it his son lay.

Took out the knife to use on his son to slay.

Abraham's faith was steady, and his faith was true.

God said, "Stop, my son. Don't sacrifice him as I told you to.

Don't lay a hand on the boy. Don't hurt him in any way.

Now I know you truly fear God. You've proven yourself this day."

Abraham looked up and saw a ram caught by its horns in the thicket.

He sacrificed the ram as a burnt offering instead of his son Isaac.

On that day, God halted Abraham's hands

Because he proved he was a faithful man.

God said, "Because you have not withheld anything from me,

Here is my promise, here is my solemn decree.

I swear by my name, here's what I will do.

I will make you many, and I will definitely bless you.

Your descendants will be numerous as the stars and the seashore sands,
All because of your obedience being a faithful and fearful man.
Your descendants will take possession of cities of their enemies.
I bless you and all nations through you because you have obeyed me.
Your bloodline will produce royalty and kings.
Your line will bring forth my son, your savior and king."

Which one of us could sacrifice our son or daughter based on faith? No questions, no protest, just pure faith. We should all learn to trust God based on this story. He will always do what's best for us, and He will test us. Will we pass the test? Especially if He calls us by name, are we ready to answer? Are we ready to stand? Let's hope so and let's pray for strength.
What impressed me the most is when God said He swears by His name. What a blessing and feeling must have come over Abraham. Truly, I don't think I could ever have the words to describe this blessing. Keep allowing God to bless you and keep reading His Word.

Genesis 22 (entire chapter)

War in the Womb

Abraham said to his oldest servant, "Put your hand under my thigh.

Swear to the Lord of heaven and earth you will find my son a wife.

God said of my offspring, 'All this land shall be thine.'

Find my son a wife, and you will be free of the oath of mine

But if she will not follow, don't take my son back there."

With his hand under his thigh, he said, "Abraham, I do swear."

The servant set out to the city of Nahor to complete his task.

He prayed to the Lord, for he knew Abraham's faith was steadfast.

Rebekah gave the servant water, and this is when he knew

Without hesitation went back to the well for his camels more water, she drew

Without question, he knew he had found Isaac's wife.

Then he asked, "Is there room for us to spend the night?"

He gave her arm bracelets weighing ten shekels and a golden earring.

Rebekah ran quickly and told her mother's household about these things.

Her brother Laban prepared the house and food for him to eat.

He gave him straw and fodder for the camels and water to wash his feet.

"I will not eat until I tell of the errand my master gave to me.

The Lord of heaven blessed Abraham with flocks, herds, gold, and donkeys,

So deal loyally and truly so that I may turn to the left or to the right.

Look, Rebekah is before you. Take her to become Isaac's wife."

Rebekah and her maids rose up, mounted camels, and went on their way.

Later they met Isaac, who was praying in the field that evening day.

She became his wife, but her heart was heavy, and her heart grieved.

She was barren, but with Isaac's prayer, two sons she was able to conceive.

In the womb they fought for the first son's birthright,

Not knowing this would define them; this is their lasting fight.

Like a red hairy mantle, Esau came out with hunter skills,

Followed by his brother Jacob, with his hand gripping Esau's heel.

"The older will serve the younger," the Lord said. "This is what he will do.

The struggle in your womb is not the only one nation but of two.

Their quarrel will be great for preparing food for the table,

Just as great as the first brothers, the story of Cain and Abel."

What faith Abraham had in his servant, to find his son a wife. Can you trust someone to find your children spouses? What faith he had in God. Is our faith as strong as Abraham's? Are we as diligent as his servant, not to waver or to be side racked? When you are set on a task, do you ask the Father for understanding? For wisdom? For knowledge? Sometimes, if not all, a prayer can make all the difference in the world for the task at hand. What a remarkable story of faith and trust. Another battle between two brothers, but this time they hadn't left the womb before the rivalry started. Keep reading your Bibles, and the stories of the two nations will be revealed to you.

(Gen. 24:1–4, Gen. 24:12–14, Gen. 24:18–22, Gen. 24:28–34, Gen. 24:49, Gen. 24:59–61, Gen. 25:21–26)

Brother's Deceit

Isaac said, "Easu, take your bow and go out to hunt game for me
Let me bless you. Prepare it how like it, so I can eat.
I want to give you all my blessings before I die."
But Rebekah told Jacob because he was the apple of her eye.
She convinced Jacob and commanded him to obey.
"Let your curse be my curse." Rebekah could not be swayed.
With food prepared, as Esau, Jacob she did dress.
With Isaac almost blind, she knew he would pass the test.
On Jacob she placed animal skins on his hands and neck.
Deceiving Isaac, Jacob entered the tent to be blessed.
Isaac asked, "How did you find the game so quickly?"
Jacob lied and said with success, "The Lord wants you to bless me."
"Your hands are like Easu, but your voice is that of your brother."
Half-blind, Isaac didn't bless the son being deceived by the other.
When Easu entered the tent, he said, "Father, please bless me."
Isaac knew he got deceived and started to tremble violently.
Hearing his father's words, Easu let out a great and bitter cry.
"Away from the fatness of the earth and away from the dew of heaven's high."
These were Isaac's words as Easu lifted his voice and wept.
"You shall live by the sword but break Jacob's yoke from your neck."
Rebekah told Jacob, "Easu is planning to kill you one day.
Go to live with my brother until his fury turns away."
During the time with Laban, God sent him into a dreamlike state.
God said, "You will be different once you are fully awake."
Jacob traveled and came to the land of the east.
He made a vow with God, a promise he had to keep.
This was the journey, the beginning and his start.
This was the journey that changed Jacob's heart.

Deceit, deception, and lies can destroy a family to its core. Sometimes the truth can be just as damaging, but at least it is the truth. Which would you prefer? What makes this sin far greater is that she not only deceived her stepson Esau but her husband Isaac as well. Do we have alternate motives? Do we speak the truth or seek to deceive people? What would you do for your child? Would you stand by them whether they were right or wrong? Will you stand by Jesus? Does He stand by you? Truth is the same today as it will be tomorrow or in the far future. The truth never changes, and neither does God, because He is the truth.

(Gen. 27:2–4, Gen. 27:5–10, Gen. 27:13, Gen. 27:20–24, Gen. 27:30–34, Gen. 27:38–40, Gen. 27:42–45, Gen. 28:10–22)

Birth of the Twelve

Jacob was in love with Rachel at first sight.

For seven years he worked, but it seemed like overnight.

He had to marry Leah because of the custom where he lived.

Another seven to work for Rachel until Laban could he give.

During this time, Leah felt that she was not loved.

However, she was blessed with seven children from God above.

Altogether, Jacob was blessed with thirteen children,

And Rachel had two sons named Joseph and Benjamin.

Four sons were conceived by the servants of the wives.

This total conception created Israel's twelve tribes.

These are the children of Jacob, including his wives and their servants he had children with:

Zilpah (Leah's servant)—Gad and Asher;

Leah—Reuben, Simeon, Levi, Judah, Issachar, Zebulun, and Dinah (daughter);

Rachel—Joseph and Benjamin;

Bilhah (Rachel's servant)—Dan and Naphtali.

The fathers of the twelve tribes committed a great many sins against others and each other. Their birth and beginning is a bloody tale, but God blessed them, forgave them, and watched over them. Please read some of the stories I left out to better understand the twelve tribes of Israel's journeys—journeys of deception, blood, murder, and disobedience to God.

In Genesis 30, you can read how God blessed Jacob, and he became a wealthy man by tending to Laban's flocks. God didn't let Laban's flocks increase because he was mistreating Jacob. Also, Genesis 28–30 is the story of Jacob meeting his wives and their sibling rivalry, which passes on to their children and their rivalry. Remember Jacob had sexual relations with four women, and two of them were sisters. Could you share your bed and husband with your sister? Could you share your husband with three other women? An even bigger question: how did Jacob keep the peace?

Deception to Forgiveness

"Jacob, go back to the land of your fathers, and I will be with you.

I am your Lord; therefore, you know my words are true."

"We must leave because Laban's attitude has changed against me.

He changed my wages ten times, and God has not allowed him to harm me.

God has taken his livestock and has given them to me."

"I am the God of Beth-el where you made a vow to me."

Jacob packed everything and headed to the land of Gilead.

Laban pursued for seven days because he thought he was mislead.

Laban was upset because he wanted to kiss his children good-bye.

"Don't say anything to Jacob," the Lord said to him in a dream that night.

"I am searching for a household God that I cannot find."

"Remember the women are my daughters, and all that you have is mine.

So let's set this pillar and heap between you and I,

That no harm comes between us, and neither of us will cross this pillar's side."

That night they feasted, and Laban stayed by Jacob's side,

The entire time, Jacob was worried about being viewed in Esau's eyes.

With gifts sent ahead, Jacob prayed to the God of Abraham and Isaac.

Jacob thought his brother was still angry and afraid of his attack.

He put space between the herds because he thought death was his fate,

Divided his people into two groups, fearing attack, thinking one group could escape.

Because of his fears, Jacob stayed alone in his camp that night

And wrestled with a man he couldn't overpower until the daylight.

"You have struggled with God, with humans, and you have overcome.

I will not tell you my name, but I will bless you, my son.

From Jacob to Israel you will be called from this day.

I have been with you, my son, and I have heard you pray.

You have been face-to-face with God, and I have spared thee.

I have transformed you, changed your name. Now continue your journey."

When he met Esau, they embraced as brothers, and they wept.

When they were last together, all Jacob had was a staff when he left.

Esau looked up and asked, "Who are all these people with you?"

Jacob said, "My wives, servants, your niece, and your nephews."

Even though Jacob deceived Esau of his natural birthright,
Esau welcomed him with brotherly love without a sign of a fight.
Back in the land where milk and honey flows.
The beginning of the twelve, and now watch them grow.

How wonderful it is to forgive your brother of his sins against you. This shows the Holy Spirit entering Esau's heart and forgiving Jacob. Can you forgive your siblings for their sin(s) against you? Don't let anger take hold of your heart because it can destroy you internally. It can eat at you for years, making you miserable. Remember the good times and love you share. The word forgiveness is powerful in its own right. We all want others' forgiveness for our sins. Please understand God loves and forgives us daily. What a wonderful God we serve!

(Gen. 31:3, Gen. 31:4–6, Gen. 31:21, Gen. 31:22–24, Gen. 31:43–49, Gen. 32:3–5, Gen. 32:6–8 Gen. 32:24–32, Gen. 33:4–7)

Baby Sister's Eleven

If you had eleven brothers and were daddy's little girl,

You would be protected at all cost until the end of the world.

And if this were you, you would be denied nothing at all,

And if in trouble, you would know which brothers to call.

Dinah, Jacob's daughter, was raped by Shechem the Hivite.

Jacob did nothing but knew her brothers would be ready to fight.

Jacob knew nothing could be done to calm some of his sons' rage,

But Hamor, Shechem's father, talked to Jacob, trying to smooth the way.

He pleaded with Jacob and his sons to find favor in their eyes.

"Please give her to me to become my son Shechem's wife.

Let us trade and live together to become as one.

Your daughter will be mine, and my son will be your son."

But the eleven's baby sister was defiled, and she was raped.

Nothing Hamor said could ease the eleven's rage and hate.

It was like telling a snake not to eat a rat

Or telling a bird, "Your best friend will be a cat."

All of Hamor's words and apologies fell on deaf ears,

The eleven watching their baby sister in pain and tears.

The brothers replied deceitfully because they had a plan.

"If you want our sister, you have to become a circumcised man.

Not only you but all the males living among you.

And if you do this, we will live in peace with you.

If not, we will take our sister, Dinah, and leave."

But Shechem was in love with Dinah, so he agreed.

Therefore, all the men went out of the city and were circumcised.

But they all missed the fire burning in the eleven's eyes.

There were only two brothers that committed the murderous acts.

Three days later while the men were in pain, the brothers attacked.

Simeon and Levi took up swords and killed every male in sight.

They knew it would be easy; no one would put up a fight.

But if you think the two brothers went too far,

The other sons came upon the bodies and looted as spoils of war.

The brothers of Dinah's vengeance weren't close to being satisfied.

They took flocks, wealth, children, and the dead men's wives.

As plunder, everything in the houses, the brothers kept.

In their minds, all they saw was their sister defiled as she wept.

Jacob told Simeon and Levi, "We are few if we have to fight,"

Afraid of the union between the Perizzites and Canaanites.

The eleven brothers stood united, and they stood strong,

Replying, "Treating our baby sister like a prostitute was dead wrong."

After this incident, the eleven went to twelve, and they increased.

Rachel gave birth to Benjamin; now the twelve tribes are complete.

With eleven sons, Jacob knew which of his sons he could keep calm and which sons would be violent. How many of us know our children's reactions to pain of their siblings? Between my brother and myself, my parents knew how we would react to horrible news. How would you feel if your sister was raped? Your daughter? Your mother? And in today's society, your brother or son? Did they follow their brothers' lead or was it a group plan? We need to be careful of smiling faces. Not all that smile have your best interest in heart. Ask God for wisdom to sift through the truth.

(Gen. 34:2, Gen. 34:5, Gen. 34:8, Gen. 34:13–17, Gen. 34:25–26, Gen. 34:27–29, Gen. 34:31)

Dream to Nightmare

Joseph's brothers already treated him poorly and mean.

The ill treatment grew worse after he told them of his dream.

Israel made an ornate robe because of the love he had for him.

His brothers knew this and did not speak a kind word to him.

He told them of the dream of his sheave rising and standing upright,

And of their sheaves gathered around his bowing in plain sight.

Because of this dream, their hatred was intense, and their anger grew.

This was something God had decreed, and it was nothing they could do.

Just as Cain and Abel, Easu and Jacob, another set of brothers, divided.

Just as the other sets, their anger and rage, they could not hide it.

His other dream about eleven stars, the moon, and the sun bowing down,

This represented his mother, father, and all his brothers on the ground.

His father rebuked him, and his brother's jealousy swelled.

Not knowing the dreams will have him thrown in a well.

Israel said, "Go check on your brothers and bring word back to me.

They're tending to the flocks and grazing them in the valley."

When they saw Joseph approaching, they said, "Here comes our prey."

Their final decision was to sell their brother as a slave.

Before that, they plotted to end his life,

Then lie to father about an animal attack happening that night.

Reuben wanted to rescue Joseph from his brothers' hands

While Judah sold him as a slave that sent him to foreign lands,

Sold to traveling merchants for twenty pieces of sliver dirt cheap,

Sold like an animal—a cow, goat, or a lost sheep.

They took a bloody robe back to Jacob for his eyes to see.

They dipped it in goat's blood, knowing father would be deceived.

Jacob tore his clothes, wore a sackcloth, and mourned for many days.

He said, "I will continue to mourn until I join my son Joseph in the grave."

Jacob had two wives who were sisters, and he also had children with the wives' servants. Did this lead to bitterness and resentment among the children? It was probably the reason for the resentment toward Joseph from his half brothers. Do you and your siblings quarrel? Is one considered the favorite? How does that make you feel? When Joseph told his brothers of his dreams, did that push them over the edge to sell him as a slave? The favorite son!

What is your brother or sister's worth? Could you sell them and then lie about their death to your father? You may not sell or siblings or plot their deaths, but do you lie to them? Do you blame them for something you did? This is the example of how not to treat your siblings. Jealousy again—Cain and Abel, Jacob and Esau. Maybe you and …

(Gen. 37:3–4, Gen. 37:5–11, Gen. 37:14–17, Gen. 37:18–30, Gen. 37:31–35)

Duty Bound

Zerah was born with a scarlet thread tied to his wrist,

But Pharez was born first; this is their birth with a twist.

At this time Judah went away from his brothers.

He met a Canaanite woman and chose to marry her.

Three times and three sons Judah's wife conceived.

Er the first, Onan, and Shelah to continue his seed,

Tamar was given to his first son as his wife,

But he was wicked and the Lord took his life.

Then Judah said to Onan, "Sleep with your brother's wife.

Give her children to raise, which is your brother's right."

But he spilled his semen when he slept with his wife.

This was wicked to the Lord, so the Lord took his life.

Judah said to Tamar, "Go live as a widow at your father's household.

You will marry my youngest son, Shelah, when he becomes old."

Judah's wife died, and he recovered from his grief.

He went to Timnath to the men shearing his sheep.

When Tamar was told, she put on a veil as a disguise.

She saw Shelah grown, and not given to him as his wife,

Tamar took off all of her widow's clothes.

She sat at the entrance on the road.

Judah thought she was a prostitute, for she covered her face.

Not knowing he would fulfill his youngest son's place,

"Sleep with me, and I'll give you a young goat," Judah said.

"Will you give me something until it arrives as a pledge?"

Judah said, "What pledge shall I give to you?"

"Your seal, cord, and staff in hand will do."

He agreed, she became pregnant, then she put on her widow's clothes.

Meanwhile, Judah sent his friend with a goat back down the road.

The Adullamite asked the men about the shrine prostitute.

"There hasn't been one." He knew Judah had been fooled.

"Let her keep what she has, or we'll become the laughing stock.

I did try to pay her with a young goat from my flock."

"Tamar acted like a prostitute," Judah was told three months later.

"Bring her out and burn her alive, because she has lost my favor."

She sent a message saying, "I'm pregnant by the man that owns these."

It was Judah's seal, cord, and staff. His eyes he couldn't believe.

Judah said, "She is more righteous than I.

I didn't give her to Shelah to become his wife."

Twin boys in Tamar's womb when it was time to give birth.

A scarlet thread on Zerah's wrist, thinking he will come out first,

But he drew back his hand, and his brother came out.

The midwife said, "This is how you have broken out!"

Did Judah leave his brothers out of guilt? And were his sons punished because of his sins to his brother Joseph? Either way, losing two sons must have been a horrible feeling. Another story of deception within the family. Do you have secrets in your family? Will those secrets eventually come to the light? This is an example to do right by God because His Will, will always be done. Something we do today can have an impact on our future, not only for us but for our children as well. Keep the faith and keep praying.

(Gen. 38)

When the Cat's Away

From the Ishmeelites, Joseph became Potiphar's slave.

His master's wife wanted to sleep with him every day.

Potiphar put Joseph in charge of everything except his wife.

Joseph knew if he crossed that line, it would be his life.

Potiphar's only concern was that of the food he ate.

Joseph handled all items, including all of his estate.

But Potiphar's wife had her eyes on Joseph every day.

When Potiphar was away, his wife wanted to play.

But Joseph refused any of her flirts and advances.

God had blessed him, and he didn't take any chances.

"Against my heavenly Father's laws, I cannot do this,

Because what you ask of me is a sin and it is wicked."

God's holy laws Joseph did not break.

To covet another man's wife would be a mistake.

Joseph stood strong, and he kept to his faith

No matter how many times it was put in his face.

She waited until the right time when they were all alone.

She could say anything, being the queen of her home.

She stalked him like a cat to a mouse,

But he escaped her grasp and ran out the house.

He ran so quickly he left his cloak in her hand,

But he also knew, *Now I am a condemned man.*

She called her servants and said, "Look, he left his cloak with me."

All a part of her plan, all part of her treachery.

When Potiphar returned, she said, "This is how the Hebrew treated me."

Potiphar was furious and threw Joseph in the penitentiary.

Just as all these troubles have come to pass,

God has a plan, and Joseph's troubles will soon pass.

The scriptures say Joseph was well built and handsome. The scripture also talks about lust, which was what Potiphar's wife was doing. She lusted after Joseph daily, and he refused daily. Could you refuse a woman's advances daily? What or who do you lust about? The flesh is weak. Amazing faith and belief in God, not yielding to temptation. She eventually lied on Joseph, and Potiphar had him thrown in prison. That was his wife. Would you not believe your wife? A hard question to answer. If Joseph had slept with Potiphar's wife, would it have been commandment seven or ten broken? Remember, rape is not always done by a man.

(Gen. 39:1–2, Gen. 39:3–7, Gen. 39:8–9, Gen. 39:11–15, Gen. 39:19–20)

Prisoner to Prince

When you are blessed by God, here's what I am told:

Everything you touch seems to turn to gold.

Just as in Potiphar's house, in prison Joseph was in charge from A to Z.

The warden had no worries because he knew God was with thee.

Two of Pharaoh's servants were imprisoned under Joseph's care,

Telling Joseph of their demise and Pharaoh's penalty was unfair.

Each servant had dreams with the symbolic number of three.

One servant's duties were restored, the other beheaded from his body.

"Think kindly of me when Pharaoh says all your duties are reinstated.

Make sure to mention me because I want to leave this place."

After two years, Joseph knew the servant forgot about his plight.

The servant was reminded when Pharaoh spoke of his dreams that night.

He told Pharaoh of Joseph and his dream interpretations coming true.

"I am sure Pharaoh, my king, he will do the same for you."

Being troubled, Pharaoh sent for the magicians and wise men of Egypt.

After failure, he sent for Joseph. "Maybe my dreams he can interpret."

Pharaoh spoke of dreams of seven cows grazing in the reeds,

The second dream of seven grains scorched by the winds of the east.

Joseph said, "Only God can open your eyes for you to see."

Pharaoh said, "But none of my people could interpret for me."

God is showing Pharaoh what He will do across these lands.

Only He can reveal this; it can't be done by any human.

Seven years of abundance and seven years of drought over the lands.

God has decided to do this with His own two hands.

He told Pharaoh of keeping a fifth to be held in reserve.

Pharaoh put Joseph in charge because it was well deserved.

"Because God has given you wisdom and His spirit is with you,

Only with respect to the thrown will I be greater than you."

Pharaoh gave Joseph a wife and a ring from his very own hand.

He had him ride in a chariot as his second in command.

A Hebrew in charge of all Egypt, unlike any other.

All of Egypt had to bow soon, just as his brothers.

Could you go to prison and keep faith in God? Would you blame Him and cut yourself off from His Word? Think about when life doesn't go according to your plans, who do you blame? Do you instead think of it as a test of faith? Does it make you spiritually stronger? We should use our lessons in life to help others when they are down or going through similar issues. We are supposed to help each other as Christians, right?

The story of Joseph's journey is one of being betrayed by his family to becoming the second most powerful man in the lands. All because of his belief in God and his unwillingness to turn his back on the heavenly Father no matter what trouble or turmoil he was put through. A valuable lesson that patience and believing God will see you through anything. We can never see what God has for us at the end of a journey, but with patience, belief, and prayer, just imagine what He will do for you.

(Gen. 39:20–23, Gen. 40:5–21, Gen. 24:9–13, Gen. 41:8, Gen. 41:9–14, Gen. 41:16–33 Gen. 41:39–40, Gen. 41:41–45, Gen. 42:6)

Feast and Famine

With seven years of famine in the land just beginning,

Jacob knew, without food, this would be his family's ending.

He sent his ten sons to Egypt for grain to buy.

"Get as much as you can; if not, we shall surly die."

All his sons left except Benjamin from his eyes.

He couldn't send him because of his son Joseph's demise.

Joseph the governor of the land sold grain to its people.

Remember Pharaoh made him second in charge without equal.

The ten brothers bowed low as they came to buy food.

Joseph spoke harshly. "Do you think we are fools?

You have come to see where we are unprotected in our land."

They replied, "Your servants were twelve brothers, the sons of one man.

One is no more, and the youngest father kept out of fear."

Joseph said, "You won't leave this place unless the youngest comes here.

Send one home, and the rest will be in prison for three days.

We will find the truth in the words that you say."

On the third day, he released them with food for their family's lives.

But Simeon was taken and bound right before their eyes.

Reuben spoke to Joseph; he was the first to speak.

Joseph turned away from them because he began to weep.

Joseph returned their silver and gave supplies for their journey.

When they stopped that night to rest and feed their donkeys,

Their hearts sank, the sight of their sliver before their eyes.

They were warned what would happen if found to be spies.

Arriving in Canaan, Jacob was informed all they were told.

He was frightened, hurt, and troubled because he was old.

Afraid, Jacob said, "All my children you take. I am deprived.

Do not take my youngest, my heart. I know I will die."

Both Reuben and Judah promised Jacob of Benjamin's safety.

One promised the life of his kids, the other, "The blame falls on me."

Their father, Israel, said, "If it must be done, then do this.

Take double sliver, the best products in the land, to him as gifts.

May God grant mercy to bring my sons back to me.

But as for me, I am bereaved. I am bereaved."

Therefore, the brothers took double back down to Egypt's land,

Bowing before their brother, at the mercy of his hand.

Joseph told his steward to take them to his house for a feast.

Horrified, they thought, *He will take our property, and we will be seized.*

They spoke to the steward about their last visit and their doubt.

Their minds were eased when Simeon was brought out.

Joseph asked about their father as he laid eyes on his brother.

He had to go in a private room to weep; he needed time to recover.

Food was served, and the brothers were seated in order of their birth line.

They feasted with him, but Benjamin's portion was greater by five times.

Would you recognize your sibling after years apart? How would you greet them? After all the years passed, the betrayal, the abuse, could you look them in the eyes? Once again, we need to take a page out of God and Joseph's book and learn to forgive. Not only others but ourselves. What are some of the lessons we can learn from this powerful story? How about the story in your life with your siblings? What have you learned or taught about loving your siblings?

(Gen. 42:1–4, Gen. 42:6–10, Gen. 42:13–16, Gen. 42:24, Gen. 42:21–23, Gen. 42:25–28 Gen. 42:35–36, Gen. 42:37, Gen. 43:9, Gen. 43:11–13, Gen. 43:18–23, Gen. 43:29–34)

Silver Lining

In the morning, they loaded their donkeys, and not gone long,

The steward went after them and brought them back to Joseph's home.

Now Joseph had a plan to bring his eleven brothers back.

He planted his silver cup in young Benjamin's travel sack.

The steward caught them and said, "Why have you repaid with an evil deed"

My master gave you food, silver, and everything that you need.

Missing is my master's cup for drinking and for divination.

Why did you take it and succumb to evil temptation?"

They replied, "He who has it will die, and we will bear the shame."

The steward said, "Very well, death, but the rest are free of the blame."

Each lowered their sacks, thinking, *This will be over quickly.*

The cup was found with Benjamin. They had to return to the city.

Before Joseph, they threw themselves on the ground and started to plea.

Joseph said, "I will keep the guilty as my slave, and the rest can go free."

Judah told Joseph the story of Benjamin and Jacob are bonded as one.

Jacob will die because this is the last of his wife, Rachel's, sons.

"I made a promise that I would bring the boy back with me.

I could not dare look upon his face of pain and misery.

Let the boy return, and in his place I will stay."

Judah pleaded to Joseph to become his humble slave.

Out of control, he removed all present, dismissed from his home.

Crying out with emotions, he finally made himself known.

"Come closer my brothers. Don't be afraid of me.

I am Joseph, your brother, the one you sold into slavery."

The enormous outcry even reached Pharaoh's ears.

Joseph wept, embracing his brothers, shedding hundreds of tears.

"Do not be distressed; this is a part of God's plan.

He has done this, and He has made me a great man.

You shall live in Goshen and be near me.

The famine isn't over. I will protect my family."

Pharaoh directed Joseph to give them carts and loaded donkeys.

He gave them clothes, silver, food, and provisions for their journey.

They returned to Jacob, and he could not believe his eyes.

They spoke of their journey and that Joseph was still alive.

They loaded all of their children and all of their wives.

Jacob was excited that he would see his son again before he died.

At Beersheba, Israel made sacrifices to the God of his father Isaac.

God said, "I will go with you to Egypt; I will surely bring you back."

God spoke to Israel clearly in a vision that very night.

"A great nation you will become, and Joseph will close your eyes."

They took a journey to Egypt totaling seventy strong.

Pharaoh gave them the best of lands they could now call home.

Pharaoh asked of their occupation, just as Joseph knew he would.

The five brothers replied, "Your servants are shepherds since our childhood."

Joseph had prepared his brothers and father ahead of time,

Just to be certain Pharaoh would not change his mind.

After Jacob blessed Pharaoh, Pharaoh asked, "How old are you?"

Jacob said, "I am 130. My years were difficult, and they have been few."

After meeting with Joseph's family, Pharaoh was happy and pleased.

Pharaoh gave them choice property in the district of Ramesses.

This was emotional for Joseph; he broke down and wept out of happiness to see his brothers. Are you distant from your siblings? Why? A misunderstanding, argument, mistrust, or numerous other things that don't have any meaning? Do you think God wants us to fight with our siblings, or anyone? Can we set aside our pride and apologize for any wrongdoings? We must also remember the apology must be sincere and from the heart; otherwise it is meaningless. What are the two greatest commandments Jesus teaches us?

(Gen. 44:1–2, Gen. 44:4–13, Gen. 44:17, Gen. 44:18–33, Gen. 45:1–8, Gen. 45:16–22, Gen. 46:1–4 Gen. 46:8–26, Gen. 46:33–34, Gen. 47:7–10, Gen. 47:11)

Pharaoh's Wealth

In Egypt and Canaan, the famine continued as Joseph degreed.

He sold grain for money and put it in Pharaoh's treasury.

The Egyptians' money was gone. Joseph said, "Bring me all your livestock."

In exchange for food, he took cattle, horses, their herds, and their flocks.

This managed to sustain all of the people for another year.

But what will happen, because the famine was so severe?

"We have nothing else. We gave our livestock and all our monies.

Please let us live. We will give our all our lands and our bodies.

We offer our land and ourselves as slaves in exchange for food.

Just give us grain that we may live and our land doesn't become destitute."

Pharaoh's wealth prospered greatly because it was in Joseph's hands.

Pharaoh now had all the money, the livestock, and all of Egypt's lands.

Joseph had a plan; he told the Egyptians he had an offer and a deal.

"I bought you and your lands. Now I will give seed to plant in the field.

The seed that you plant will produce during the time of harvest.

Remember this is a gift. Pharaoh's share of the harvest will be one fifth.

Now look how wealthy Pharaoh has become

By a former Israelite slave that's not his son,"

This Israelite, appointed by Pharaoh, all the Egyptian lives he saved.

In the book of Exodus, how did the Israelites become Egyptian slaves?

During this time, people were desperate for food, so they sold anything they had, including themselves. What would you sell to survive? Your body? Your soul? What are we selling now? We may say to ourselves, "I would never do that," but when we are faced with starvation, we might do things differently. Remember we have to walk in someone else's shoes before we judge. A very old saying is "all money ain't good money." If money controls you, do you hurt others to obtain it? How about your family? Do they suffer because you are chasing money?

(Gen. 47:13–15, Gen. 47:16–17, Gen. 47:18–21, Gen. 47:23–25, Gen. 47:26)

Blessings and Death

Jacob, at 147 years old, knew it was time to die.

As God degreed, his son Joseph would close his eyes.

Calling all his sons together, Jacob said, "Gather around me.

These are my last words, so allow me to give my blessing to thee.

Reuben, my firstborn, my might, my strength excelling in honor,

You are as turbulent as the waters; you will excel no longer.

You defiled my couch, for you went to bed with my wife.

You will be first no more, at least not in my life.

Simeon and Levi, let me not join their counsel or their assembly.

They murdered men in anger and crippled oxen as they pleased.

Judah, your hand on the neck of your enemies, and your brothers will praise you.

You are a lion's cub, and your father's sons will bow down to you.

He will tether his donkey to a vine.

He will wash his garments in wine,

Like a lion he crouches, and he lies down.

The scepter won't depart until he comes who wears the crown.

Zebulun, my son, I will give you this gift.

You will live by the seashore to become a haven for ships.

Issachar, you're a sturdy donkey, noticing how pleasant is his land.

Bending his shoulder to the burden, submitting to labor by another's hand.

Dan will be a snake beside the road, a viper along the path

That bites the horse's heel so that the rider falls back.

Gad will be attacked by a band of raiders,

But at their heels he will attack these invaders.

Asher's food fit for a king; shall his delicacies be.

Naphtali bears beautiful fawns like a doe set free.

Joseph, a vine that archers attack and shoot at him with hostility.

His arms stayed limber and his bow remained firm and steady

Because of Jacob, the rock, your father's God helps you.

Because the almighty God, the one who is blessing you,

The prince among his brothers, on his head let these blessing rest.

Reaching heights of eternal hills, blessings of the womb and breast,

Benjamin is a ravenous wolf. In the evening his plunder he divides.
In the morning devours his prey. Now it's time to close my eyes.
Now take me to my ancestor's burial site,
The cave Abraham bought from Ephron the Hittite."
The twelve tribes of Israel, Jacob said good-bye to each with a message,
Finished his charge, drew in his feet, and joined his ancestors in death.

What will be your last words to your children? Will you bless or curse them? Do you know your children as well as you should? We all want the very best for our children, the same as God wants the best for us. The amazing point is that God forgives. Do you? Don't go to your deathbed without forgiving and asking for forgiveness.

He even speaks about Jesus in verse 10 to his son Judah. Some of his sons had notable descendants, such as:

Levi—Aaron, Moses, Eli and John the Baptist
Dan—Sampson
Naphtali—Barak and Elijah
Gad—Jephthah
Joseph—Joshua, Gideon and Samuel
Benjamin—Saul, Esther and Paul
Judah—David and Jesus.

(Gen. 49:3–4, Gen. 49:5–7, Gen. 49:8–12, Gen. 49:13, Gen. 49:14–15, Gen. 49:16–18, Gen. 49:19, Gen. 49:20, Gen. 49:21, Gen. 49:22–26, Gen. 49:27)

There are more stories in **Genesis** that I didn't write about. Stories, such as the Tower of Babel (Gen. 11), Ishmael's descendants (Gen. 25), and many more. Please pick up your Bible and read; this is the only way to gain understanding of His Word. Even while you are in church, will you take the pastor's word on everything or will you verify for yourself what are God's words? The last thing I will do is try to keep you from Gods temples, but are all clergy people honest? Just watch the news and you can answer that for yourself. I am only asking that you read and verify Gods words, not humankind's words.

The next series of poems are prayers, before we start the book of Exodus. We all need the power of prayer in our daily lives. Some of us have the feelings of hopelessness or suicide, or just the feeling of loneliness. Please understand God will never leave you. You can leave

God, but He will not leave you. There is nothing you can do to make Him love you less or more. He loves us, period! Every day He opens your eyes, you are given the opportunity to change anything in your life, if you believe. Ask yourself one question, and you will have your answer: is there anything God can't do?

In the book of Exodus, I will attempt to give you poetry on an amazing period in the lives of the Israelites. Can you imagine actually being a witness to the miracles performed by God? I was always in awe of the lack of and strong faith during the time God actually was with the Israelites. The parting of the sea, all the plagues that struck Egypt, manna, water from a rock, and the Ten Commandments! How could you not have faith? A cloud by day and fire by night. We don't have these types of miracles today, but our faith should not be swayed or diminished.

We should thank Him every day for what He has given us that we take for granted. Your shelter, food, job, car, eyesight, touch, and I can go on and on. We should feel blessed daily that the Father awakened us this morning. Please understand I am not a saint, I have my battles, and I fight daily to keep the faith. This is a process and journey to God, not a quick fix. I sincerely hope you enjoyed the first section about Genesis and that you have your Bible with you.

Dear Father

Family/Friends

Heavenly Father,

Please help my family and friends.

Under your protection,

Lead them to the Word.

Help them to love each other.

Guide them to your teachings.

Nurture them with your spirit.

Keep them from harm.

Please let them prosper.

Give them insight into your Word.

Give them wisdom.

Give them guidance.

Teach them how to help others.

Let them be a light to guide others.

Most of all, Father,

Let your will be done.

In Jesus's name,

Amen.

Love

Keep my spirit open to love.
Keep my heart open to love.
When you send her my way,
Keep my eyes open.
When you send her,
She will come with love,
Your love,
Your spirit.
Keep us in prayer.
Keep us close to you.
Let us be one
With you,
With your spirit,
With your love.
Your love never fails.
Your love is everlasting.
Dear Father,
Keep my heart open to love.
In Jesus's name,
Amen.

Gifts

I thank you for my gifts.

These are your gifts.

Bless me to share these gifts,

Give back to you, Father.

I am honored.

I am blessed.

Please allow your gifts

To benefit others.

I am humble.

I am grateful.

Your gifts are wonderful.

Your gifts have blessed me.

Let these gifts bless many.

In Jesus's name,

Amen.

Mercy

I come to you today
As a sinner,
Asking for mercy,
Asking for grace,
Asking for your blessings,
Asking for wisdom,
Asking for understanding
To let your will be done,
Asking for humility
To let you take control,
Asking for appreciation.
Your Son died for me.
He died for us.
Bless me, Father.
I am a sinner.
I need your mercy.
I need your grace.
I need your love.
I need You.
In Jesus's name,
Amen.

Forgive

Allow me to forgive,

First forgive myself

For all my transgressions,

For all my sins.

Allow me to forgive

My enemies

Or those who I think are my enemies.

For all that I wronged,

All who have wronged me,

I need forgiveness.

For the kingdom,

For those closer to me,

Those harder to forgive,

My friends,

My family,

My coworkers.

These are hard.

You have forgiven me

All my life.

We took your Son,

And you still forgave.

That is our example.

Soften our hearts.

Heal our souls.

Allow us to forgive.

In Jesus's name,

Amen.

Alone

Today I just feel.
I feel desperate.
I feel overwhelmed.
Some days I'm tired,
Tired of fighting,
Tired of people.
To be a better Christian,
It's a battle,
Some days a losing battle.
Today, Father,
I feel drained.
I feel hopelessness.
Today, Father,
I feel alone.
Father,
Today I have tears.
I have pain.
Today, Father, sin is calling.
My internal struggle,
It's raging.
Today, Father,
I just feel.

Unworthy

Dear Father,
Today I am blessed
Because of you, dear Lord.
Today I am humble.
Today I am grateful.
All I have I owe to you.
Without you I have nothing.
With you I have everything,
All the blessings and all the grace.
I am unworthy.
It is more than I dreamed,
More than I deserve.
I do not care about what I don't have
But am grateful for what I do have.
I am in awe of your magnificence,
This incredible journey you've taken me:
How many times you saved my life;
How many times you've given me grace;
How many times you kept me on the path;
How many times you gave me strength.
This is why I'm humble.
This is why I'm blessed.
This is why I feel unworthy.
You are an amazing God.
I thank you.
I love you.
Amen.

When I'm Weak

Father, give me strength
When I am weak.
Temptation is all around.
Evil seeks to destroy me.
I need you more when I'm strong,
To keep me strong
When I am weak.
The strength you give me,
I can help others.
We can lean on each other
When I am weak.
I know you love me.
I know you won't leave me.
I know you watch over me
When I am weak.
Amen.

The Lord's Answer

"You have a woman,

But you must cherish her.

You have money,

But you must spend it wisely.

You have a heart,

But you must open it to love.

You have clothes,

And you were brought into this world naked.

You have food,

Yet some starve.

You have shelter.

My temple is always open.

You have everything.

You have me."

Thanks

I come to you humbly,
Asking you to touch my heart,
Asking you to touch my spirit,
Asking you to touch my soul.
I am coming to you thankful,
Thankful for people that dislike me,
Thankful for people that hate me,
Thankful for people that gossip about me,
Thankful for people that lie on me,
Thankful for people that try to keep me down,
Thankful for people that put up roadblocks.
I thank you for these people
Because it gives me the opportunity
To show forgiveness.
It allows me to show your love.
It allows me to show what a Christian is.
It allows me to show character.
It allows me to show faith.
It builds my strength.
It builds my foundation.
Most important, it tightens our bond.
Father, I am asking to keep your spirit with me.
In Jesus's name,
Amen, amen, and amen.

A Prayer for Freedom

What keeps me going every day?
The light of the Lord to light the way.
The thought of rejoining my family.
They have my body, but my mind is free,
Free to go deep into my subliminal,
Free to not think about being a criminal.
New choices, new times, and new faces.
Better decisions, better thinking, and new places.
This is the spirit of God in me.
With open arms, I let it flow freely,
Free in my mind, body, and soul.
I give in, Lord; now you have control.
Guide me in your righteous path.
Show me the blessings that you have
For me, even though I have sinned.
With you at me side, I know I will win.
This is my prayer on bended knees.
Guide my path when I'm set free.
I know you haven't forsaken me.
I thank you for what you have done for me.
With eyes open, I am waiting to see
All the blessings you have in place for me.
Yes, I am in a place I don't want to be,
But soon I will be where God wants me.
Until then, I will wait patiently.
Soon my mind and body will be free.
Amen.

Exodus

River of Death and Life

"I am Pharaoh, the king of all these lands.

My word is supreme; every knee bends on my command.

I don't know Joseph's generation of past days.

I know the Israelites will all remain my slaves.

If war breaks out, will they join our enemies?

I'll put slave masters over them, and they'll work for me.

I will have them build Pithom and Raamses, two more of my cities.

I'll make their lives bitter, with harsh labor working them ruthlessly.

As my slaves, I must attack them at the core. I will advance my fight.

The vigorous Hebrew women give birth before the midwives arrive.

Shiphrah and Puah, kill every boy born. These are my decrees."

But they feared God more than Pharaoh and spared the male babies.

The Israelites continued to grow in power and continued to multiply.

Shiphrah and Puah have families now because God blessed the midwives.

To all the people, this is the order Pharaoh gives:

Throw the male babies in the Nile and let the slave girls live.

Pharaoh's cruelty has already caught God's eyes.

Pharaoh forgot about the Israelite that saved Egyptian lives.

Soon one will come to set the Israelites free.

With God's help, he will take them out of slavery.

The same river Pharaoh ordered all male babies to their end

Will give birth to Moses. This is where his story begins.

Many generations have passed, and the current Pharaoh knew nothing about Joseph and how he saved all of Egypt. With Joseph being the second in charge over all of Egypt, why wasn't there any recorded history about him? After all, he did save Egypt. Was it because he was an Israelite? Or was it because his Pharaoh changed his name to Zaphnathpaaneah (Gen. 41:45)?

The building of Pithom and Raamses cities were store/supply cities for Pharaoh. The building of these cities brought on the horrible injustices to the Israelites. Think about the slavery of black people during the eighteenth and nineteenth centuries in America. There must have been killings, rape, senseless beatings, and many more atrocities. The times we are faced with the most disparity of our lives are the same times we need to lean on Jesus more.

(Exod. 1:8–10, Exod. 1:11–14, Exod. 1:15–22, Exod. 2:2)

Prophecy

For three long and hard months, a mother hid her child.
She had to. Pharaoh's orders were to throw them in the Nile.
With a papyrus basket, she coated it with pitch and tar,
Placed in the Nile, but the basket didn't get very far.
Pharaoh's daughter saw the basket among the reeds.
She opened it and felt sorry for the infant male baby.
With his sister watching, keeping an eye on her brother,
She approached the princess, hiding in the reeds' cover.
Pharaoh's orders ended, being a blessing, not a curse.
Moses was taken back to his mother to become his nurse.
Moses was the name given, adopted by the princess,
Given back to her to be raised in the palace,
Which means he was educated, fed, and in good health.
He received the royal treatment with riches and wealth.
Being adopted by Pharaoh's daughter, what would you expect?
For him to do slave labor with chains around his ankles and neck?
God placed Moses right where He needed him to be,
The other side to prepare him to set the Israelites free.
As a man, Moses killed an Egyptian and hid him in the sand.
News got back to Pharaoh; now Moses was a wanted man.
Being careful, Moses thought no one saw him the other day.
Breaking up a Hebrew fight, one said, "Will you treat me the same way?"
Reaching Pharaoh's ears, Pharaoh tried to have Moses killed.
Moses escaped to Midian, and soon the prophecy would be fulfilled.

What would you do to save the life of your child? To what extremes would you go? Can you put him/her in danger in order to save them? Could you bear not knowing their fate? How do you feel not knowing where your child is?

Why did Moses kill the Egyptian? Did God put this in his heart about the abuse of his people? Here's a thought: he was raised as Pharaoh's grandson, and did Pharaoh's daughter try to stop Pharaoh from killing Moses? Or because of his order of killing all Israelite males play a part in wanting Moses death? After all, Moses wasn't a true Egyptian, being a distant heir to the throne.

(Exod. 2:2–4, Exod. 2:5–10, Exod. 2:11–14, Exod. 2:15)

I Am

In Midian by a well, Moses was resting his feet.
He rescued seven daughters' flocks of the local priest.
Invited by Reuel because he saved his daughter's life,
Reuel gave him Zipporah to become his wife.
Years passed, and the king of Egypt died.
God continued to hear the Israelites outcry.
God knew this was the time to act.
His vow to Abraham, Isaac, and Jacob, His solemn pact.
At Mt. Horeb, God appeared as a burning bush in Moses's path.
Moses went to go see the flaming bush that fire seemed to last.
"Moses, take off your sandals because holy ground is this place."
Afraid to look at God, Moses hid his face.
"I am sending you to Egypt to set my people free.
I will give them spacious land flowing with milk and honey.
I have come down to rescue them from Egyptian hands,
And I will guide you, Moses, to the promised land."
Moses said, "Who am I to go to the Israelites and lead?"
God said, "When you bring them out, worship here as I decree.
Worshipping on this mountain that I sent you will be a sign.
Moses, be patient. Leading them here will take some time."
God said, "I Am who I Am.
The God of Isaac, Jacob, and Abraham.
Tell the elders I Am has sent me to you.
Don't fear, Moses. I will tell you what to do.
Tell them to do sacrifices on a three-day journey.
I will strike the Egyptians so hard they'll listen to me.
You will plunder the Egyptians when you depart.
Your hands will be full of riches, and so will your carts."

We often feel unworthy of God's blessings, but that is when we should listen to the Father. He did not bless you for nothing; he gave you a blessing worthy of what you have done or about to do. We may not know or understand at the time of the blessing, but God does. In the scriptures, Reuel's name, we later find out, is also Jethro.

(Exod. 2:15–17, Exod. 2:20–21, Exod. 2:23–24, Exod. 3:2–3, Exod. 3:5–6, Exod. 3:8–10 Exod. 3:12–14, Exod. 3:16–22)

Displeasure near Death

Moses was convinced this task was too big to complete.

God had to show Moses miracles to put him at ease.

"On the ground, throw your staff."

It changed to a snake, and Moses jumped back.

God said, "Grab it by its tail and watch it closely.

"To a staff again it changed. Do you have eyes to see?

Place your hand in your cloak and listen to me.

Now pull out your hand infested with a skin disease.

Now place your hand back inside.

It's healed. Do you now believe your eyes?"

"Lord, what if they say, 'The Lord didn't appear to you'?"

"If they don't believe the two signs, here's what you do.

Take the water from the Nile and pour it on the ground.

The water you take will turn to blood on dry ground."

Moses, not convinced, still had his doubts.

God said, "Who gave the human beings their mouths?

Don't worry about being slow of tongue and speech.

I will send Aaron with you, and he'll be your mouthpiece."

God was angered and said, "I will instruct the both of you.

Take your staff and perform the signs I have shown you."

"Returning to Jethro, asking permission to go where God sends me."

Jethro said, "Go, my son, with your family and go in peace."

Later at a lodging place, God was about to take Moses's life.

Zipporah cut off her son's foreskin with a flint knife.

And with it, she saved his life by touching it to his feet,

Saying, "Surely you are a bridegroom of blood to me."

After that, the Lord let Moses be.

He met Aaron and continued on their journey.

The same is true today. How many miracles must God perform before we believe? God made our mouths, minds, hearts, and everything that we are. Why wouldn't Moses believe that God would give him the words? Does God send you on a task, and you have doubts? Should we not believe that if He sends us on a task, everything we need He will give to us?

Moses learned a valuable lesson, that disobeying God can be more dangerous than dealing with Pharaoh, who did not believe in God. We keep repeating the same lesson; believe in God first, and you can't go wrong! Trust the Father. He doesn't do anything half-right.

(Exod. 4:1–7, Exod. 4:8–9, Exod. 4:11, Exod. 4:14–17, Exod. 4:18, Exod. 4:24–27)

Busin Bricks

Moses and Aaron went to Pharaoh and said, "The Lord said let my people go."

Pharaoh said, "Why should I obey? Because your God I do not know.

Why are you stopping all the people from doing their task?

Because of your interference, I will break their backs.

I will no longer supply straw for making daily bricks."

"Go and get your own straw wherever you can find it.

You must complete all the work that Pharaoh requires."

This is what Pharaoh commanded to all the slave drivers.

"Complete the quota of bricks as yesterday and for today."

Israelite overseers asked, "Why do you treat your servants this way?"

"Make the work harder to keep them from Moses's lies.

The work remains the same no matter how much they cry."

God keeps His promises from the very start.

He told Moses He would harden Pharaoh's heart.

Why would Pharaoh let the lazy Israelites go free?

They were building his cities with labor easy and free.

"Moses, why did you put this trouble on our heads?

You put the sword in their hands, now Pharaoh wants us dead."

These were the questions by the elders after the meeting they had.

"Pharaoh called us lazy and talked about us extremely bad."

Moses returned to the Lord and had questions of his own.

The Lord said, "Relax, because I will bring my people home.

Because of my mighty hand, Pharaoh will drive them out the country.

I was not known by your forefathers, but now my people will know me.

I am the Lord, and under the Egyptians, their yoke I will break.

I will redeem you with an outstretched arm; this is the oath I take.

I am the Lord."

Pharaoh had an enormous ego, which was understandable in Pharaoh's eyes. He was the ruler of all the land; no one could be mightier than he. Why should Pharaoh yield to a Hebrew God when he thought he was a god? If you had the power of life and death, would you yield? So he thought ...

This time the Lord revealed His name—Jehovah (Exod. 6:3). Do you think the Lord spoke to Moses more sternly this time? Once again the same lesson: trust God first, especially if He calls you by name! Will you obey if He calls you by name? Are you too busy in your life not to listen when He calls?

(Exod. 5:1–2, Exod. 5:4–7, Exod. 5:10–14, Exod. 5:15–16, Exod. 5:20–21, Exod. 5:22, Exod. 6:2–8)

Diamond Hard

"Your brother Aaron will speak for you.
Your Lord, your Father, will tell you what to do.
Pharaoh will ask you to perform a mighty task.
You will perform the miracles by using thy staff.
God and Prophet will you be in Pharaoh's mind.
I will harden his heart and multiply my signs.
The two of you will go before Pharaoh to speak."
Moses was eighty, and Aaron was eighty-three.
Aaron threw his staff down, and it became a snake.
Pharaoh said, "That's no miracle; that's a piece of cake."
Pharaoh's wise men, sorcerers, and magicians performed the same,
But Aaron's swallowed up their snakes and changed the game.
Pharaoh hardened his heart and would not let the Israelites go.
God said, "Perform this in front of his officials. I want all to know.
Confront Pharaoh in the morning on the Nile at its bank.
When the waters change to blood, be assured this isn't a prank.
Water will be blood in every vessel of wood and stone.
Let my people go. I need to bring my people home.
The fish in the Nile will die, and the river will stink.
The water will be blood, and no Egyptian will be able to drink."
But Pharaoh himself was not the bit impressed.
The magicians did the same and relieved Pharaoh's stress.
To get water, all the Egyptians had to dig along the Nile.
Pharaoh didn't take it to heart and went back to his palace in style.
God said, "Let my people go, so that they may worship me.
If you refuse, I will send a plague of frogs on your entire country.
Tell Aaron to stretch his hand with the staff to make the frogs rise.
They will be in your ovens, bedrooms, troughs; there is nowhere to hide."
Once again the magicians did the same by their secret arts,
But this time Pharaoh said, "I will let your people depart."
Moses said, "Set the time that all the frogs will be gone except in the Nile."
Pharaoh said, "Tomorrow," saying it with a twisted smile.

The frogs died, and they were piled into heaps.
Only frogs in the Nile lived, but the entire land reeked.
Pharaoh hardened his heart because he saw there was relief.
Pharaoh was still convinced not to let the Israelites go free.
The Lord said, "Aaron, stretch your hand out with thy staff.
Strike the dust on the ground, and the dust will become gnats."
Pharaoh's magicians tried to produce the same feat,
But it was God's miracle, and they yielded defeat.
The magicians said, "This has got to be God's hand."
Pharaoh still would not let them leave the land.
After the Nile, frogs, and gnats had passed by,
The Lord said, "Now I will strike them with a horde of flies.
I will make a great distinction in tomorrow's sign.
I will deal differently between your people and mine.
Moses, go to the Nile and tell Pharaoh my words are true.
'Let my people go or I will deal harshly with you.'"
All of Egypt was covered with flies by the might of God's hands.
Pharaoh said, "Go and sacrifice to your God in these lands."
Moses said, "That's not right because the Egyptians will stone us.
We need a three-day journey to the wilderness as God commands us."
Pharaoh said, "I will let you go. Now pray for me."
But in his heart, Pharaoh answered deceitfully.
"Pharaoh, because you have not changed your mind,
I, the Lord, have set a time.
This time tomorrow, all the livestock in the fields shall die.
But my children's livestock has favor in my eyes.
This is the fifth time Moses my servant asked you to set my people free.
Now five times my holy power and five times my holy fury."
And Pharaoh's heart grew hard more five times.
None of the Israelites' animals died; his investigation could not find.
How much longer could Egypt hold steadfast?
But God knew how long Pharaoh's anger would last.
God told Moses and Aaron to go to the furnace and get some ashes.
"Toss the ashes the air and watch how it affects Pharaoh's masses.
Festering boils will be on man and beast alike,
All to bear witness to my holy power and might."

The boils were on all the Egyptians and on all the magicians.
They couldn't stand before Moses, and Pharaoh would not listen.
God told Moses to confront Pharaoh. "And this is what you will say.
'Let my people go to worship me that I may show them the way.
This time my full force to show that there is none like me.
I will send hail like none before; there is nowhere you can flee.
You set yourself against my people and will not let them go.
This hailstorm will be the worst, bringing pain, misery, and woe.
Every beast and man not brought in will perish.
Your losses will be great, including all things that you cherish."
The Lord told Moses, "Stretch your hand toward the sky."
The Lord rained hail throughout Egypt all day and all night,
But no hail fell in Goshen where the Israelites dwell.
Lightning flashed back and forth, and it continued to pour hail.
Again Pharaoh lied, saying, "We have sinned, and we are wrong.
I will let you go. Take your people and go home."
Moses said, "The thunder and hail will stop when I leave the city."
God said, "How long will you refuse to humble yourself before me?
Let my people go or I will send locusts unlike you have ever seen.
They will eat all left from the hail; nothing left will be green.
They will cover the ground until it turns black."
This is the Lord's great plague of locust attack.
The Lord told Moses, "Stretch out your hand for my locusts to come eat.
I will bring the east wind throughout the day to invite my locusts to a feast."
Pharaoh's officials asked, "How long will this man be a snare to us?
Let them go, or do our counsel you no longer trust?"
Pharaoh said, "You are bent on evil if I let you go.
You can only take the men, not the young or the old."
Moses said, "We must all depart because the Lord we will celebrate.
Women, children, flocks, sons, and daughters, all of this we will take."
After the locusts devoured Egypt and had their all-day feast,
Pharaoh asked Moses, "Have the Lord take this plague away from me."
The Lord changed the wind west and took the locusts to the Red Sea.
Not one locust was left, not one that an eye could see.
Like a diamond, one of the hardest substance known to man,
Pharaoh's heart was hard and would not let them leave the land.

The Lord told Moses, "Stretch your hand out and hear what I say.

Egypt will not see the light of the sun for the next three days.

It will be so dark the people will not see their hand to their feet.

But my people will have light, a sign that they will soon be free."

Pharaoh said, "Go but leave your cattle and herds of all kind."

Moses said, "No, we all go; not one hoof will be left behind."

With his heart hardened, Pharaoh told Moses to leave from his eyes.

"The next time you appear before my face, you shall surely die."

The Lord told Moses, "This is my last plague to show my awesome might.

I will strike down all of Egypt's firstborn during the hour of midnight.

From the mighty Pharaoh down to the son of the female slave,

All the firstborn cattle, none will escape. Only my people shall I save.

There will be a wailing in Egypt that will last for all time.

Among the Israelites, not a dog will bark because these people are mine."

In anger, Moses turned and left from Pharaoh's sight.

He had to summon the elders and explain Passover's night.

"The Lord's Passover meal must be eaten with haste.

For generations to come, this day you must commemorate.

Place lamb's blood on the top and both sides of the doorframe.

After the destroyer leaves, Egypt will never be the same.

During the midnight hour, God did all that He has said.

Egypt's wailing was great, not one house without someone dead.

Pharaoh told Moses, "Take the Israelites and go, but please bless me."

The Egyptians urged the people to hurry and leave our country.

After 430 years, the descendants of Jacob left Egyptian lands,

Not by Pharaoh but the power of Jehovah's hands.

During the time Moses was told to go to Pharaoh to let God's people go, God displayed His power and might, a small fraction of what He can do. All He said He would do happened just as He said. One of the truly amazing things God did was to harden Pharaoh's heart to display to the rest of the world that He is the one and true God of heaven and earth. How arrogant Pharaoh must have been to think he could stand against God. But if and when you read the scriptures, you will notice that Pharaoh asked to be blessed or prayed for on more than one occasion.

How could you not have undying faith after the power of God shown right before your eyes?

What miracle are we witnessing today? Do you believe? How strong is your faith? No, we don't see the seas being parted or a pillar of fire, but does that means God is not with us? Think about the miracles God has done for you. Has He saved your life? Our faith should be just as strong if not stronger because we have a blueprint of what to and not to do.

(Exod. 7–12)

Song of Deliverance

"What have we done by letting all the slaves get away?

I will hunt those Israelites down until the end of days."

Pharaoh harnessed his chariots that were six hundred strong.

With armies in pursuit, he knew it wouldn't take long.

Pharaoh close, the Israelites knew in the wilderness they would die,

Telling Moses they were happier as slaves, living a better life.

The Lord asked, "Why are you crying to me with tears?

My glory will be displayed through Pharaoh and his charioteers.

The armies of Pharaoh you see today you will see no more.

My power I will display will be like none you have ever seen before.

Moses, pick up your staff and raise your hand over the sea.

I will part the waters, and dry land will be beneath your feet."

With a strong east wind, the sea opened with water walls on both sides.

Again God showing his might, with Israelites not believing their eyes.

The Lord confused the Egyptians, making their chariots hard to navigate.

The Egyptians shouted, "Let's get out of here, the Lord fights in their place."

"Moses, raise your hand over the sea again when my people are safe."

As Moses raised his hands over the sea, the waters rushed back in its place.

Not one survived of Pharaoh who chased the Israelites to the sea.

The Israelites were in awe from the power the Lord had unleashed.

The people of Israel walked through the sea on dry ground.

They prayed, worshipped, and sang the deliverance song.

The whole community of Israel journeyed to the desert of sin.

And this is where more complaining to Moses picked up again.

"In Egypt, our pots were full with bread and tasty meat,"

The Israelites complaining about the food they had to eat.

The Lord said to Moses, "I will rain bread from heaven for you.

Follow my instructions. Here is what you will do,

The people are to go out and gather enough for just that day

And twice as much on day six because the seventh is a holy day.

I have heard the grumblings of the Israelites.

You will have all the meat you can eat at twilight.

In the morning, I will give bread for your bellies to be filled.

Know that I am your Lord, and this is my divine will."

So many quail came and covered the entire camp at twilight.

A layer of dew in the morning, his people never saw such a sight.

The Israelites had to ask Moses, "What is this?"

Moses said, "It's the bread from God as a gift."

It was difficult for Moses to understand,

His people not being grateful for food from God's hands.

Some kept manna till morning, and others gathered on Sabbath Day.

This disobedience had Moses speechless without a word to say.

The Lord asked Moses, "How long you will refuse my instructions?

Not obeying me will certainly cause the Israelites destruction.

From Egypt I brought you out and delivered you.

Now I am giving heavenly manna to sustain you.

An Omer of manna was placed with the law of the tablets,

To be placed before the Lord for all generations not to forget.

The Israelite ate manna forty years given by God's hands,

Until they came and settled on the border of Canaan lands.

Pharaoh and his officials did not want to give up his cheap labor. Do you think you could be a happy slave? After the miracles being witnessed against Pharaoh, would you still have doubt in God? Would you keep complaining? Are we doubting and complaining today about the smallest of things? Instead of complaining, we should thank Him for His blessings.

The manna God gave to his children had to have all the nourishment needed for any human. God doesn't do anything half-right. The food you receive from God, do you complain bitterly or do you thank Him? Think about the many people who will not eat today or for days. Do you complain about eating chicken every day, just as the Israelites complained about eating manna? The point is you're eating, yet some people starve to death. What are their complaints?

(Exod. 14:5–7, Exod. 14:10–12, Exod. 14:15–18, Exod. 14:21–22, Exod. 14:24–25, Exod. 14:26–28, Exod. 15:1–20, Exod. 16:1–3, Exod. 16:4–6, Exod. 16:11–13, Exod. 16:20, Exod. 16:27–28, Exod. 16:33–35)

The Fear of God

In the third month, they camped in the wilderness of Sinai.
The same day the Israelites escaped Pharaoh's slave life,
God called Moses up the mountain, saying, "Come speak with me.
I have much to discuss and much shall I show thee.
You've seen what I did, and I bore you on eagle's wings.
Therefore, if you listen to my voice, you will have an understanding.
Keep my covenant, and you will be a special people to me.
You will become a holy nation and a kingdom of priests."
Moses gathered the elders and spoke God's words true.
The people answered together, "All God says we will do."
God said, "I will come in a cloud, and all will hear what I say.
They will have no doubt in you forever from this day.
Now, go to the people and for two days you will consecrate.
I will descend on this mountain, and it will tremble and shake.
Set bounds for the people as to not touch the mountain's base.
If so, they will be put to death because this is a holy place.
They shall come near the mountain when the trumpet sounds long.
If not, they will be shot by arrows or they shall surely be stoned.
This includes all man and all beasts; are all the same.
Once you warned them, you no longer have the blame."
Moses went back down the mountain and got the people sanctified.
"Be ready for the third day, but don't come near your wives."
On the third day, the Lord descended on the mountain in fire.
The trumpet was very loud, and all the people trembled for their lives.
A thick cloud on the mountain with thunder and lightning,
Smoke like a furnace, the mountain shook. It was very frightening.
The Israelites said, "Moses, you speak with us, and we will hear."
Moses said, "God has come to test you. You have nothing to fear.
His fear may be before you, so that you may not sin.
He has love for His people; now keep that within."
Now soon before the phrase "the fear of God" was instilled,
God called Moses up the mountain to discuss the children of Israel.

The saying that says putting the fear of God in you,
Now you know because you've seen what God can do.
God with own voice gave Moses the Ten Commandments
To give to His beloved people, another sign of His covenant.

How amazing and frightening this must have been. The entire mountain shook violently. An entire mountain! With fire, thunder, lightning, and a trumpet! Would you have been afraid or praised Him? Either way, what an event to have witnessed. And to hear God's voice! This is where *I believe* the phrase "put the fear of God in someone" originated. He showed His power, His voice. Mountains shook, with thunder, lightning, and a very loud trumpet. Need I say more?

(Exod. 19:1–2, Exod. 19:4–6, Exod. 19:10–19, Exod. 19:21, Exod. 20:18–21)

Exodus 20—The Ten

You shall have no other gods before me.

I am the only God you shall bend your knee.

You shall not make idols.

These are my words in my Bible.

You shall not take the name of the Lord your God in vain,

Which means you shall not say it in shame.

Remember the Sabbath Day and keep it holy.

This is the day that is meant for me.

Honor your father and mother.

They gave life; there are no others.

You shall not kill.

My vengeance will be real.

You shall not commit adultery.

Be happy with the one that married thee.

You shall not steal.

Items not yours should have no appeal.

You shall not bear false witness against your neighbor.

Be honest is all I am asking for.

You shall not covet.

Enjoy what you have without regret.

The scripture in italics is what *Jesus said*. Please look at those scriptures. We are not in the New Testament, but Jesus's words on the subject could not be omitted.

How many worships Satan or any other God? No other God! Luke 16:13

How many of us have idols? We love money, sex, clothes, and fame and try to replace God with them. We don't start off by putting things before God, but it just kind of happens. We need to be mindful of the time devoted to these things and pray for strength. Matt. 4:10

Substitute someone you love name with God, then use it as curse or slander or derogatory. Probably wouldn't feel good. Then why do it to God? Why abuse His name? We should not take lightly His name because one day we will answer for it. Matt. 5:34

The Sabbath Day. We can use this time to thank God for life. Use it to rest and reflect and to give Him the honor He deserves. To refresh our spirits. To uplift others. To study His Word. I can keep going, if you understand now what His day can represent. Mark 2:27–28

Honor the people that gave you life, your father and mother. We may not always see eye to eye with our parents, but that is not a green light to dishonor them. Parents have a special place in God's eyes. There is a promise attached in the scriptures (Exod. 12). Matt. 10:37

Murder! Can we kill someone with words? In our minds? Matt. 5:22

Adultery of the mind and lusting after another person in our thoughts. Is that adultery? Or only the committing the physical act makes us guilty? Matt. 5:28

Stealing. Why? Work for what you want. Be diligent in your efforts. Would you want someone to steal what you worked for? *Matt. 5:40*

Bearing false witness. Does that mean not getting involved or telling half the truth? How about just a plain lie? Does this apply only to a court system? At home, at work, in your heart? The truth will always be the truth even if it's told days, weeks, and years from now. The truth is constant, and so is God. *Matt. 12:36*

To covet. Sometimes we may covet in the mind, but we need to take a closer look at why. Is it a deeper reason why we covet? Is it not fulfilling a basic need? Is it resenting the fact that we don't have what someone else has? Ask God for that basic need and help with that resentment. *Luke 12:15*

We have not begun to read the New Testament, but it is very important to read what Jesus says about the commandments.

Guardian Angel

"I am sending an angel ahead of you to guard you along the way,
Looking after you to bring you to the place I prepared for you to stay,
He is my angel, and with him my name is within.
He will not forgive your rebellion or tolerate your sin.
I will oppose all that oppose you, and they will be my enemy.
Do all what I say to do and listen to him carefully.
Don't bow down before their gods or follow their practice.
Break their sacred stones to pieces; everything you must demolish.
I will take away all sickness from among you.
There is nothing your Lord cannot do.
None of my people will miscarry or be barren in your land.
You will live a long life; I will give you a full life span.
I will make all your enemies turn their backs and run.
The fear I'm sending will be as terrorizing as the sun.
My angel will go ahead of you and bring you into the lands.
Blessings will be on your food and water given by my hands.
Every nation you encounter I will confuse and send into dismay.
The Hivites, Canaanites, and Hittites will get out of your way.
I will send hornets that will drive out the people in fear,
But I will not drive them out in less than a year.
I don't want the land to become desolate with numerous beasts.
This will take time because I want your numbers to increase.
I will establish your borders from sea to sea,
My covenant with Abraham as far as his eyes could see.
With Isaac and Jacob, you will be as numerous as the sands.
The people who live here, I will deliver them unto your hands.
With these people you must not make an agreement.
They will turn you from me, causing much resentment.
Do not let them live in your land to cause you to sin against me.
Remember I am your Lord God; I am the one who delivered thee.
Soon I will confirm my covenant with laws and commandments.
This land I am giving to you will be my lasting testament."

God is amazing. Would you think about worshipping another God after all you have seen your God do? Are you? Remember, you can't serve two Gods, and He is a jealous God. Sometimes unknowingly we place "things" in the place of God, such as money, fame, cars, and the list goes on. What do you place above God unknowingly? Once God makes a covenant, He keeps it. We are still descendants from Abraham. Do think God has broken His word? Why should we?

(Exod. 23:20–22, Exod. 23:24–26, Exod. 23:27–30, Exod. 23:31–33, Gen. 15:17–20, Gen. 17:19, Exod. 2:24)

History Lesson

God told Moses, "Go back down. Your people are in danger."

What Moses saw made him have rage and anger.

"After everything our God has done for you to see,

You make false gods and still you don't believe.

From the time I sent Moses to Pharaoh to set you free,

The time my staff changed to a serpent and ate Pharaoh's three.

From the time blood ran from the mighty River Nile

To the time I sent frogs to cover the land mile by mile.

From the time I sent gnats from the dust and the massive fly swarm,

But none of my people or animals, not a hair on them was harmed.

The more I put on Egypt, the more Pharaoh hardened his heart.

Then I gave Egypt more plagues to have Pharaoh let you depart.

I gave the livestock a plague and boils on animals and people alike.

Then a hailstorm as none before to show all the land my holy might.

I sent locusts on the land to devour all that survived.

After that I sent darkness over the land to cover the sunlight.

After three days, Pharaoh told Moses, 'When you see my face again, you will die.'

Then I sent my destroyer to kill all firstborn during the hour of midnight.

With lamb's blood on your posts, my destroyer didn't touch what was mine.

Remember this Passover from every generation, a law for all time.

I heard your cries, and I listen, and I know all of your fears.

Still no faith in me when Pharaoh's chariots attacked from the rear.

Between you and Pharaoh, I placed a pillar of my holy fires.

Parted the sea with dry ground to walk and a water wall on both sides.

Once you crossed and I knew all my people were safe,

Moses raised his hands again, and I put the water back in its place.

Afterward you sang, prayed, and worshipped me,

And still you have little faith in me.

I sent you quail and manna daily for you to eat.

I had my heavenly cloud to shield you from the desert heat.

And when you complained about water and dying from thirst,

I made water come from rock because I put my people first.

I gave you Joshua and a strong army to command.

He struck down the Amaleks as my strong and powerful right hand."

Now back down the mountain, listening to all God has told,

Moses saw their sins and the false calf god made of gold.

He smashed the tablets at the mountain's foot and didn't know what to think.

Moses burned the golden calf, ground it to powder, and made the Israelites drink.

Moses said, "Join me all that have the love of the Lord from within.

All others, the Levites will strike down because of their sins."

The Lord said, "I have set you apart as my special people to me.

All on earth is mine, but you are my holy nation and kingdom of priests,

So lead my people from the bonds of rejection and from slavery

To my land I promised, flowing with milk and honey.

How mad would you be after speaking with God to see your people having a party? And worshipping a calf! Really. Again, God is slow to anger. Do you think God let Moses handle this situation because He had not given them the laws yet? Which side would you have chosen? What do you worship? When we receive a blessing from God, do we immediately turn away from Him? Sometimes we have a habit of having a short memory or selective amnesia.

Stiff Neck

"If I traveled among you starting on this day,

You are a rebellious people, and I would destroy you along the way."

The Israelites went into mourning and removed their fine clothes and jewelry.

Moses had to go to the Lord and present a humble forgiveness plea.

"You did not bring us out to wipe us out,

But now we understand what our Lord is all about.

You told me to bring your people to the promised land.

You dealt with our enemies, delivering them to our hands.

'I know you by name' is what you told me

But did not say whom you will send with me."

The Lord said, "I will go with you and give you rest.

Obey my instructions, and you and my people will have the best.

I will do what you asked because you have found favor in my grace.

I will pass before you, but you will not see my face.

I will place you in the cleft of this rock.

While my glory passes, don't be afraid or go into shock.

I will place my hand over you until I pass by

Because if you see my face, you shall surely die.

Now chisel out two tablets like the first made of stone.

My people will carry them to the place I made them a home.

In the morning, come up the mountain and present yourself.

No flocks will graze here. Come alone, by yourself."

Moses went up the mountain with two tablets in his hands.

As the Lord descended in a cloud, Moses bowed, a humbled man.

The Lord, slow to anger and abounding in love,

The compassionate and gracious God, His name itself is love.

"Go with us, your people who are stiffed neck.

Take us as your inheritance and forgive our wickedness."

The Lord told Moses, "I am making a covenant with you today.

My work for you will be awesome if you learn to obey.

Remember the Lord your God; jealous is my name.

Worshipping another god, my wrath I have you to blame.

Your enemies I will drive out and deliver them to you.

I brought you out of Egypt; there is nothing your God can't do.

Smash their altars and stones and hear me when I call.

Making treaties and sacrificing with them will be your downfall.

The firstborn offspring of every womb belongs to me.

No one is to appear before me with their hands empty."

For forty entire days and forty entire nights, which was Moses stay

Without food or water, Moses listened to the words God had to say.

Down from the mountain with the covenant law in his hands,

Moses was not aware that he was now a changed man.

Everyone ran from Moses when they saw his face.

His face shone after his stay being in God's grace.

Moses gathered the people and spoke on God's behalf,

Giving the Ten Commandments, the covenant that will last.

How many chances did God give them to clean up their act? How many has He given us? Are we still going against God's plan after all the forgiveness He blesses us with? By now we should see a pattern to follow His instructions, and we can't go wrong. He tells us that He will bless us abundantly; just listen and obey. As imperfect humans, it is difficult for us to give up control of our lives, but with prayer and faith, it can be done. Difficult but attainable. In time, the process becomes easier with God's help. He wants this for everyone, to see His kingdom.

(Exod. 33:3–6, Exod. 33:12–14, Exod. 33:18–23, Exod. 34:1–3, Exod. 34:4–8, Exod. 34:10–16 Exod. 34:19–20, Exod. 34:29–35, Exod. 35:1–3)

I hope you enjoyed reading Exodus poems. The next series of poems are personal prayers and poems about life and a preview of poems to come. I know you still have your Bibles with you, and you have been referencing the scriptures at the end of the poems of Exodus.

Leviticus will only be one poem. This book of the Bible I will not attempt to write about His instructions or offerings but will start again in the book of Numbers. Please enjoy God's Word in your Bible that you can understand and gain wisdom in His Word. God wants us all to make it to heaven. Do you want to be saved? Are we doing God's work? We all can do better; we all have to make changes in our lives. The journey will have trouble, headaches, turmoil, and tears, and at times we will want to quit. But if you think about it, the journey will have joy, tears of happiness, love, friendship, and many blessings. God never said the path is easy, but there is a path. And at the end of that journey is everlasting life with God. That sentence is joy itself! God is great.

Poems

My Oath

Now that I'm totally free,
My family has welcomed me.
This is the type of love I need,
The type of love meant for me.
My eyes are open, and I can see
The path God has laid down for me,
The path and direction at my feet,
The path of Jesus and His spirit in me.
So I pray for His guidance and His wisdom
To keep me straight to see His kingdom.
My family I will not hurt a second time,
And with their strength I will stay in line.
I am free, and I am out.
This time there is no doubt.
I will honor the freedom Jesus gives to me.
I will honor His will and honor my family.

First Stone

From Genesis to 2 Timothy,

My Jesus is coming to set me free.

From coast to coast and all over the land,

The Bible talks about the evil and wickedness of man.

I stand before you because I am not exempt.

I have sinned and done evil when my heart had contempt.

Just as in the days of Noah, people were full of sin.

Just as today, this is the time Jesus will come again.

I am not a prophet; you don't have to believe me.

Just sit on your couch and turn on your TV.

You say, "How can you preach with all the sins you've committed?"

I'm not, but the Bible gives you all the tools to be equipped,

Tools He gives for your salvation and everlasting life,

Tools for you, your neighbor, your parents, your kids, and wife.

This is my closing; now I'm about to bring it home.

Don't judge me, for those without sin …

Cast the first stone.

His Place

We all sometimes get depressed,
And sometimes our words can't express
Our feelings we have in our mental state.
And sometimes our minds take us to a dark place,
A place of pain, suffering, and strife,
But God can grant you a new life,
A life that won't have you feeling down and out.
Now let me tell you what God is all about.
He is about joy, happiness, and love,
Come on and listen about the one true God above.
All the sad and unhappy feelings you have today,
With one word God can take that all away.
All He has to say is, "Make it so."
Are you in the same place from a year ago?
Most of us aren't in the same place from last week.
God is faithful; all His promises He always keeps.
The promise of love and keeping us in His heart,
The promise that His love will never depart.
Remember we are all a part of the human race,
But God can take you to a better place,
A place of no pain, no grief, and no sorrow,
A place where you don't have worry about tomorrow.
This is the place where we all need to belong
A place where God says, "Rest, you are home."

Lighted Path

God's delay is not God's denial.

He is working for you, so it may take awhile.

I know He has many blessings for me,

So I will sit in his waiting room patiently.

He is working on my situation for me.

Most of the time, He works on the patience in me.

Sometimes it's the character of others to help me,

Or it could be the Holy Spirit to help guide me.

God only asks, "That you love and believe in me,

That I will give you all the blessings that you need.

To make a giant oak, it takes an entire century,

And overnight for a mushroom. How can you not trust me?

Have faith and trust because your blessings are about to begin."

Understand the delay because God is glorified in the end.

We learn that while we wait, we experience soul and body rest,

But prepare yourself because sometimes our faith is put to the test.

We must plan on preparing for our blessings from the very start.

Look at Noah, Abraham, Moses, and David, a man after God's own heart.

If they took things in their own hands, where would they be?

Maybe like Sarah and the reason for turmoil in the Middle East.

If there isn't a lesson, how can you teach?

If there isn't a test, how can you have a testimony?

The only point I am trying to say:

Be patient and let God light the way.

The point of this piece is to understand that patience is essential when dealing with God. He answers prayers when the intent and motives are true. He may not answer when you want Him to but rather when He knows you are able to handle the gift He gives you. Sometimes we are not mentally ready for the prayers we want. God waits until you are in the best state of mind and when other vital insights are revealed to you. This can take years or a lifetime. Just remain patient. In other words, get out of God's way.

Legal Issues

How uncomfortable do you feel in a courtroom?
Waiting for sentencing, thinking that you're already doomed,
Thinking, *With all the evidence they have on me, I can't win,*
Because the prosecution has pages and pages of all my sins.
Will my attorney make a plea deal to come to my aid?
I'm not worried about any fees because with His blood He already paid,
But the evidence is very heavy, and the evidence is complete.
The Judge knows all, and He can't be deceived.
Even when I thought I was hidden and out of sight,
The Judge said, "Everything in the dark will come to the light."
He has evidence from when I was just able to walk,
Evidence about the language I used when I was able to talk.
He has evidence when I cheated, made mistakes, and when I lied,
Things I did when I thought I was away from seeing eyes.
The prosecutor keeps piling more and more evidence on.
My attorney takes my hand and says, "Be calm, my son."
The prosecution has more evidence on my entire life,
When I committed pain, misery, and strife.
The judge reads off ten laws that I didn't abide by.
In my heart, I know this is the end of my life.
But my attorney informed the Judge that I'm ready to make a plea.
"Your Honor, my client is humble and sorry for having contempt of thee.
He is ready to give his heart and soul to me.
We have touched his spirit, and he is ready to be complete.
Father, look at the prosecutor. He already thinks he can win.
And he's right; none of my clients have lived without sin.
He has been fighting us since the very beginning.
He's as stubborn as a mule, but he knows his time is ending,
All of my clients have repented, and all have prayed.
I ask only for your mercy and for your grace.
Father, I am your son. You know the pain that I embraced.
Father, I was mortal and died so that they can be saved,
And because of that, Your Honor, I rest my case!"

In God We Trust

We see Him every day on this planet Earth.

We see Him when a mother gives birth.

There was a time unknown was His name,

Disgracing Him, giving Him nothing but shame.

So wicked, He gave His laws to us,

Writing them down, to humankind did He entrust.

Simple rules to follow for our souls to win.

We failed, so His Son died for our sins.

Faith and saving our souls is what we should live for,

That maybe one day we will see our creator.

Spin It (To Positivity)

No matter how much negativity,

No matter the haters,

No matter the naysayers,

Spin it.

Find positive in negative.

Feed off of the haters.

The opposite is yes.

Spin it.

I didn't pass a test;

Study more.

I didn't get the job;

Rewrite the resume.

I didn't get the promotion;

Work harder.

Spin it.

The hard part:

Change your mind-set.

One way to change:

Prayer.

Spin it.

I took a setback;

It was a setup for a comeback.

I lost everything.

So did Job.

Spin it

With faith.

He as well as you

Can get double.

Spin it.

Faith.

Heaven and Hell

There are many interpretations of heaven.
I wonder if I will make it to heaven
To see things that were lost long ago,
To talk to people that you only read about,
To play with animals that would eat you whole.
Maybe I'll have wings and fly with angels,
Even sit and talk philosophy with God.
If not, hell here I come.
Does the devil really have horns and a tail?
Or is he a smooth operator?
Will I be forever in flames and eternal heat?
Or is it one big party?
Either place I go,
Life as I know it is gone.

Leviticus

The book of Leviticus is a handbook for the priests, Levites, and Israel, giving them an outline and understanding of their duties. Leviticus also informs the Israelites how to live. God gives instructions on health, offerings, prayer, worship, and more about Him. How can you have a better blueprint on life than to have it given to you by the Lord? God wanted the Israelites to be a nation of priests and an example for all the world. Before they could be an example to the world, God instructed them on how to be that example. Every offering, festival, and sacrifice was holy because God is holy.

God gave a detailed outline on what was to be sacrificed and how the priests were to carry out their duties during these times. Again, how can you go wrong with the greatest of all teachers? God did not want His people to fall back into idol worshipping or living the way other nations lived. This is why the Lord gave instructions on how to live. How many times in Leviticus did God remind the Israelites, "You must be holy because I am holy"? He gave instructions on what to eat, conduct, diseases, and even sex. God created sex, but we sometimes use it not in its intended purpose. He is concerned about our sexual habits and sexuality. Do we acknowledge God with our sexuality? Or is it perverted? Remember sex is a private celebration, not a social media, public domain, exploited event.

The Lord gave instructions for punishing disobedience as well. During these times, the punishment sometimes was death or being cut off from the community. These were needed to keep the community whole and to prevent sin from taking over. Again, "I am holy, so you must be holy." These harsh penalties were to prevent disease, pagan worship, immoral practices, and many other detestable acts against God and the community. As a parent, God wanted His children to succeed. Is it any different from any parent today? We want the best for our children and community and give discipline when disobedience occurs. The only poem I write about in Leviticus is the death of Nadab and Abihu, Aaron's sons. Please read the entire book of Leviticus and enjoy His words. My reoccurring theme—please get a Bible that you can understand, and we will learn and grow together with God as our guide. He is our teacher and example for healthy living, spiritual growth, justice, and many more things on our journey toward eternal life. The two greatest commandments are to love God and to love your neighbor as you love yourself (Matt 22:36–40).

I Am Holy

"I am holy,

So you must be holy."

Moses anointed Aaron and his sons as God commanded.

Their anointing to serve as priest, as God had planned it.

Moses consecrated them and washed them from head to feet.

Moses ordained them to be the first order of priests.

With all the precise instructions about the offering,

Why would Aaron's sons take it with less meaning?

Each offering was given great detail,

Guidelines for the priests not to fail.

"I am holy,

So you must be holy.

I gave you instructions on how to perform your duty,

And this is how you disrespect me?"

Aaron's sons were to continue the priestly bloodline.

This was to be with their family for all time.

"After my blessings and instruction,

You caused your own destruction.

You were ordained and set apart

But had contempt of me in your heart.

Between my people and me, you stood in the gap.

You were their bridge, their guide, and their map.

Because of your disobedience

I must display my holiness.

I am holy,

So you must be holy.

I am holy, so they must die.

I destroyed them with a blast of fire.

This is what happens when you are careless.

This is what happens from your lack of awareness.

I have given you the honor and responsibilities

To perform sacrifices as my holy priests.

Now my holiness is on display.

You were in position to light the way."

Aaron was silent.

He knew what this meant.

As a father, it hurt,

But they had to serve first.

"I am holy,

So you must be holy."

Moses told Aaron not to show grief,

"Or God will punish the entire community.

Make sure you don't uncover your hair,

And your clothes, do not tear.

You will die if you leave the entrance of this place.

Remember your sons. Don't make the same mistake."

"I am holy."

Did Aaron's sons Nadab and Abihu become careless? Did they forget their teachings from God? How often do we forget to show the proper respect to God? Do we get into a routine and not show reverence? But being the first order of priests, we would think they would have cared about their duties and taken them more seriously. Sometimes it's hard to be the first. The first sets the tone, makes the example for others to follow. Think about how God took time in the explanation of His work to be priests. Should our ministers, pastors, and leaders of our churches have any less care? Do they? The bigger question is, will God hold them less accountable than Aaron's sons or us?'

(Lev. 8, Lev. 10:1–3, Lev. 10:6–7)

Haikus

These poems are kind of in the Japanese style haiku but not officially. The traditional style haiku are about two subjects, separated by punctuation, seasonal preference with double meaning, unexpected perspective, seventeen syllables, and generally about nature. I decided to keep the seventeen syllables but spin it about God and keep the 5-7-5. The 5-7-5 format is the first line with five syllables, the second with seven, and the third with five. They have a different style with a different vibe but still the same meaning of God's love. Please continue to read His Word as much as you can, hopefully daily, and continue to read *four* pages per day in a Bible that you can understand. It makes a difference when you can understand what you read and enjoy it.

Peace/Joy

The sounds of the Lord
Are in my heart and my soul.
Such a joyful sound.

War/Lost

In heaven was war,
But God's angels stood their ground.
The devil lost all.

Near/Now

Please hear my prayer.
Please give me your blessings now.
The devil is near.

Love/Divine

God's love is divine.
Each person from His own heart,
His love never fails.

Day/Pray

What a day to smile.
God's love is all around us.
What a day to pray.

Blood/Grace

The blood of Jesus,
The life giving of His grace,
Joy of His mercy.

Death/Love

He died for us all.
How can we not love Jesus?
He can save us all.

March

Six days they marched
With the sound of the ram horns.
Jericho walls fell.

Stand Up

Stand up for the Lord.
He died to save all of us.
Stand up for the Lord.

True

The Bible is true.
The last days are upon us.
Get your soul ready.

Selfless

Will you save your friends?
Their souls need saving as well.
Think of others first.

One or Two

Love them as yourself,
This is one of God's commands,
Others before self.

First/Last

Those who are first, last.
There is a meaning with this.
Those who are last, first.

Down

The pride of a man
Having his nose in the air
Can bring down a man.

Foundation

Standing by his side,
The ever-faithful woman,
Foundation of man.

Point

When you judge others,
Where does your finger point to?
Others first or self?

Signs

Heed the warnings signs.
Jesus Christ is very close.
Get your soul ready.

Path

With God, there is light.
He will show the way to life.
His Son is the path.

Two

Journey to Jesus.
Love Him as you love yourself.
Now love your neighbor.

Sing

When do angels sing?
When a soul gives up to Christ,
You can hear their songs.

Waters

Rejoice with Jesus.
Baptism in Christ waters.
Let your soul be His.

Time

The devil is mad.
The Redeemer fights for us.
His time will end soon.

Give It

Our path should be clear,
The only way to heaven.
Give your soul to Christ.

Trust

Why do we test God?
Maybe our faith is not strong.
Pray to God for strength.

Kin

Love all your siblings.
One day they will be long gone.
You will mourn for them.

Right

Give parents respect.
After all, they gave you life
By keeping you safe.

Love

The love of my life
Should be Jesus, my Savior,
Creator, and God.

Tempt

Temptation of flesh,
I need my armor on now.
My flesh is so weak.

Best

My mom is the best,
We talk about Jesus Christ.
We both love Jesus.

Numbers

Curse of the Womb

"If her impurity is undetected
And her faithfulness is suspected,
The feeling of jealousy that she is impure.
Take her to the priest to test her to be sure.
Have the priest stand her before me
To determine if her husband has been deceived.
She will present a grain offering for jealousy.
The bitter water will put a curse on thee.
This curse will cause your abdomen to swell.
Your womb will miscarry if the truth you do not tell.
Loosen her hair and place in her hands the reminder offering.
This is the test for truth if she was a faithful queen.
In the bitter water, wash in the scroll curse.
If she is guilty, this will cause her pain and hurt.
The priest will place her under oath and say,
'This water will bring a curse if you have gone astray.'
Dust from the Tabernacle floor the priest will take.
Pour it into the Holy water with a jar made of clay.
Then the woman is to say, 'Amen, so be it.'
This is when the priest will tell her to drink it.
If she is guilty, the curse will run its course.
The husband will be innocent of wrongdoing without remorse.
The woman will bear the consequences of her sin.
If innocent, she will be able to have the gift of children."
These laws were in place to serve the entire community,
To keep them from detestable sin and rampant disease.

Jealousy is not anything new, especially with marriages. Even today, priests and pastors give counseling to married couples who have lost their faith in each other. We should stop flirtatious behavior and build the bonds with our spouses. Sometime the accusation or the perception can be worse than the act. The emotional negative perception can leave internal scars to last a lifetime. We need to remember to love and cherish our spouse every day. We should maintain the things we did while dating to attract our spouse; that should be maintained while married. We should grow and communicate together to strengthen our bonds. Do all you can *not* to lose your trust with each other.

(Num. 5:11–13, Num. 5:16, Num. 5:19–23, Num. 5:31)

Ask and Receive

Even when you destroyed some with your eternal blaze,

They came to me stop it, so to you Lord I prayed.

I did not give these people life,

But I put up with their whining and strife.

Why are you treating your servant so harshly?

Please, God, have mercy on me.

We want meat to eat as they come whining to me.

If this how you intend to treat me, then go ahead and kill me.

God's manna looked like small coriander seeds.

Where can I get meat for all these mouths to feed?

There are too many with hunger that won't stop.

They won't be satisfied if we slaughter all herds and flocks.

What can I do? The burden is too heavy on me.

God, do me a favor and spare me of this misery.

Why did you tell me to carry them like a mother carries her baby?

How can I carry them to the land flowing with milk and honey?

God said, "Gather seventy men, and I will come and talk to you.

Has my arm lost its power? Is there anything I cannot do?

They will bear the burden of the people that exist.

I will place on the seventy some of the same Holy Spirit.

Purify yourselves, for tomorrow you will have meat to eat.

You will have so much you will be sick of it from head to feet.

I've heard my people outcry to gorge themselves with meat.

Your whining has been heard, and you shall receive."

For miles in every direction, the Lord sent quail

As if they were on overnight delivery by mail.

"You have rejected me.

Now I will discipline thee.

While still in your mouths and going into your belly,

I will strike you with a plague and a horrible disease.

Next time, take special care for the desires you ask

Because you could receive the power of my full wrath."

How upset God must have been with these stiff-necked people? He was providing them with everything. Manna from God. I'm sure it provided them with all the nutrition needed because He doesn't do anything half-right. There are lessons to learn from this: the tongue, contentment, greed, lack of faith, and many more. Moses must have felt overwhelmed and underappreciated. Can you feel the weight on Moses's shoulder while reading this in Numbers? What do you do when you feel exactly like Moses? Do you pray for strength, guidance, and wisdom to get through your trials? As a Father, God gave his children needed discipline. Many had to pay the price for their lust and desires. They paid with their lives. Again, trust God and you can't go wrong. Even further in the Word, read Psalms 78:25–32. We all know the old saying, be careful what you ask for, you might just get it! We should ask for more of His Spirit to stay and get on the path He wants us to follow.

(Num. 11:1–3, Num. 11:11–15, Num. 11:18–20 Num. 11:21, Num. 11:24–25, Num. 11:31–35)

Simply Put

Miriam and Aaron spoke against Moses because of his Ethiopian wife.

Their brother, Moses, many times saved their life.

God said, "Come out of the tent, the three of you.

Aaron and Miriam, step forward. I want to talk to you."

In a pillar of cloud, at the tent's entrance, God stood.

He made His words clear and plain, and they understood.

"When there is a prophet among you, I speak in visions.

I am the Lord thy God. This is my decision.

In all my houses, my servant Moses has faith,

That's why I speak to him face-to-face.

Why then were you not afraid to speak against my servant?

Because of this, my anger you cannot prevent."

As the cloud lifted and God began to go,

Miriam's skin was leprous; it turned as white as snow.

Aaron said to Moses, "Against you we have sinned so foolishly."

"Please, God, heal her," Moses cried out with his plea.

God said, "If her father would have spit in her face,

Would she not have been seven days disgraced?"

For seven days outside of camp, Miriam was confined.

The people did not leave for seven days' time.

Afterward, the camp moved to explore Canaan.

God told Moses to send scouts to report on the land.

This is a short chapter but has an incredible meaning. Should we question God's appointment to others? Why did she? Was she punished because she was the lead instigator? Aaron wasn't punished. How much of Moses's faith in his siblings diminished? We do know Miriam isn't mentioned much after this until her death. This is a familiar story with jealousy and craving more than what God has given you. Jealousy! Should we not concentrate on the gifts He gives us instead of the gift of others? From poet and prophetess to having leprosy, this must have been a humbling experience for Miriam. During these times, people shouted, "Unclean!" and ran the other way. What was her feeling during her seven days of exile? What fear Aaron and Miriam must have had when

God called them to the Tabernacle. Remember in Exodus, this is the same sister that saved Moses at the Nile, and now he had to save her. We should all be careful and aware of sibling jealousy and rivalry. We need to uplift our brothers and sisters, not tear them down. This short chapter is very powerful.

(Num. 12)

My Choice

"Why did you set yourselves above the Lord's assembly?

The Lord is with them. The entire community is holy."

These were the words that passed through Korah's lips.

Moses fell facedown in grief when he heard this.

"The Lord will show who belongs and who can come near.

You Levites have gone too far, and you have no fear.

The Lord has separated you from the other Israelites.

To work in the tabernacle and to minister, only you Levites.

Tomorrow we will let the Lord God decide our fate.

Put coal in your incense, and before the Lord you will place."

Dathan and Abiram would not be summoned by Moses like slaves.

"No we will not come. Who are you that we should obey?"

Moses angry, said to God, "Do not accept these men's offering.

I have not wronged them; neither have I taken one single thing.

Each man is to take his censer with incense, 250 in all.

God will be our judge, and 250 of your followers may fall."

God said, "At once separate yourselves because this is their end."

Moses warned the community to move away from these wicked men.

"If the Lord has sent me, this is how you will know.

If He sent me, they will die naturally and grow old.

But if the ground opens and swallows them all alive,

Then you know the Lord God is standing by my side."

As Moses finished, the ground split and took them to their doom.

Holy fire came from the Lord, and the 250 men were consumed.

The earth opened its mouth, swallowed them and their possessions,

Down to the realm of the dead because of their rebellious transgressions.

"Go and collect from the charred remains of the holy censers

As a reminder to the Israelites about Korah and his followers.

Overlay the altar with the remaining bronze pieces

I sign that I will not tolerate this type of disease."

The next day the community was against Aaron and Moses in opposition.

Then the glory of the Lord appeared, and this was His position.

"Get away from them so I can put an end to them immediately.
They are a stiff-neck people that have no respect for me."
A plague started to destroy the Israelites because of God's wrath.
Aaron took his censer with coal from the altar and stood in its path.
The plague stopped, but fourteen thousand people had already died.
Once again Moses made an atonement for them and saved their lives.

Moses was God's choice. Jealousy again surfaces but now by the Levites. This story is similar to Lucifer's story of wanting more power. If God gives us some kind of authority, should we not know He will bless greatly? Think back to the story of Joseph and how God blessed him! Why do we sometimes want more than what is given or blessed by God? Two very powerful words are jealousy and greed. Both can destroy a community or a family. Whatever gifts God gives us, should we not be humble and gracious for them? Are you? Sound familiar from Mariam's story in Numbers 12? A lesson that took fourteen thousand Israelites' lives for them to learn but just for that day. As we continue to read, many more lives are lost, and many more lessons are taught. We should also learn from others' mistakes and strive to obey God's words. He wants us to meet Him in His kingdom.

(Num. 16:3–4, Num. 16:7–9, Num. 16:12–14, Num. 16:15–21, Num. 16:25–30, Num. 16:31–35)

Staff and Duty

"From the ancestral tribe leaders, gather a staff, one each.
Place the names of each man for all eyes to see.
Write Aaron's name on the staff from the tribe of Levi.
I will end this constant grumbling from you Israelites.
The staff belonging to the man I choose will sprout.
After you witness this, there should not be any doubt."
Moses placed the staffs in the tent to hear God say,
"I will stop all of this whining forward from this day.
Aaron's staff sprouted from the tribe of Levi.
Put it in front of the ark so that they will not die.
Aaron, you, your sons, and family are to bear the responsibilities,
Any offenses connected with the priesthood and sanctuary.
As a gift, I am giving you the priesthood service.
If any go near the altar, both they and you will perish.
You and your sons at the altar inside the curtain will service everything.
The Levites may not go near the altar or the sanctuary furnishings.
They are to assist and join you when you minister.
Anyone who comes near, my wrath will be sinister.
Take care and follow all of my instructions.
If not, you Israelites will surely face destruction.
Remember all offerings presented to me, I placed in your care.
I give to you and your sons your perpetual share.
It is an everlasting covenant of salt for both you and your offspring.
All presented and devoted to the Lord and all the holy offerings.
Every firstborn son and unclean male animal for five shekels of silver.
Redeem them. This is your duty and your charge. You shall deliver.
Aaron, I place all these duties in your hands to care.
No inheritance of land because I am your share.
I give the Levites tithes for work in the tent they have done.
This is a lasting ordinance for all the generations to come.
Present as the Lord's portion the holiest part given to you.
Remember my words I speak and remember all that I do."

Sometimes parents have to inform their children more than once that they meant what they said. How many times must God say to the Israelites who His choices are? Will you accept God's choice if you're not in charge? Will you accept the role He has for you? Does it take a miracle for you to understand He is in charge and His words are law? Once again, Moses had to go to God about jealousy and greed from other Israelites wanting more than what God gave them. God as our parent had to reiterate His words; "Take care, follow my instructions, you are my people, and I am holy, so you must be holy." And as children, sometimes we don't listen. Are you listening to His words?

(Num. 17:1–13, Num. 18:1–7, Num. 18:14–16, Num. 18:19–25, Num. 18:30–31)

Rock of Disobedience

In the first month, the community arrived at the desert of Zin,

And the community was in opposition with Moses again.

They said, "Where is your mind that you do not think?

You led us to this wilderness with no water to drink.

Why did you bring us out of Egypt to this terrible place?

We should have died with our brothers and suffered the same fate.

You brought us here, and we have no figs or grain to eat.

We could have stayed in Egypt where we could have had a feast."

Moses and Aaron went to the tent of meeting and fell facedown humbly.

God said, "Take the staff. You and Aaron gather the entire assembly.

Speak to the rock; before their eyes, it will give water for their lives.

Follow my instructions to show the community my holy might."

With the assembly gathered, Moses had the staff in hand.

Before all, He and Aaron would follow God's command.

Moses said, "You rebels, must we bring water from this rock for you?"

But this is not what the Lord had commanded them to do.

Moses raised his arms and struck the rock twice.

Water started gushing out and saved the community's life.

With Moses and Aaron, the Lord was not pleased.

"I said speak to the rock, not to strike it repeatedly.

Because you did not listen to my command,

You will not lead them to the promised land.

For you, Aaron, Eleazar will take over all of your priestly duties.

You too, because of disobedience, the promised land you will not see.

Aaron, on the Mount of Hor, you will die,

Never to see the land of the Israelites.

Moses, across from Jericho I will allow you to see

The promised land flowing with milk and honey.

In this desert of Zin, you did not uphold my holiness.

When you join your ancestors, you have my forgiveness.

You should have continued to have faith in my presence

And not let frustration cause your disobedience."

Do you think Moses was frustrated and fed up with complaints? Do you believe because of this frustration he didn't give God credit for the water? What do you think God's feelings are? All the blessings He gives us, are you complaining? Are you ungrateful? None of the trio of siblings (Moses, Aaron, or Mariam) made it to the promised land. Why? Another lesson we should pay attention to is keeping the faith, no matter how much we are worn down. Satan comes at us from all angles: family, friends, spouses, and the community. We should pray for strength. Satan tries to frustrate us and wear us down. Please don't let this kind of persistence keep you from God. Keep your mind, heart, eyes, and soul fixed on the Father.

(Num. 20:1–13, Num. 20:22–27, Deut. 32:48–52, Deut. 34:1–8)

Sight and Voice

"Balaam, I the Lord came to you last night.
I said to go with the officials of the Moabite."
Balaam rose in the morning and saddled his donkey.
God said, "They summoned you, but you listen to me."
Balaam riding his donkey and his two servants with him,
The angel of the Lord stood in the road to oppose him,
The angel with a drawn sword in his hand ready to kill.
The donkey saw the angel and quickly turned off into a field.
Balaam beat his donkey to get it back on the road,
Thinking, *I'm the master; this donkey will do what it's told.*
In a narrow path in the vineyards with walls on both sides,
The donkey saw the angel again and didn't believe his eyes.
The donkey pressed close to the wall, crushing Balaam's foot against it.
Angry, Balaam took his staff and repeatedly his donkey he whipped.
The angel moved ahead and stood in their path in a narrow place.
The donkey lay down quietly, Balaam not knowing his fate.
Again Balaam was angry, and again his donkey he harshly beat.
"What I have I done to make you beat me?" said his donkey.
The donkey spoke, and this is what he had to say:
"Am I not your own donkey, which you ridden to this day?
I have never done this or ever given you doubt?"
The Lord with His power opened the donkey's mouth.
"No," Balaam answered, "but you made a fool of me.
If I had a sword in hand, I would kill you so quickly."
Then the Lord opened Balaam's eyes.
He saw the angel with a sword at his side.
The angel said, "The donkey saw me three times and turned away.
If not, I would have killed you and sent the donkey on its way."
Balaam said, "I did not realize you were on the road to oppose me."
Facedown, Balaam said, "I will return home if you are displeased."
The angel said, "Go with these men, but you are to listen to me.
God is not done with you; this is the first part of your journey."

Are we sometimes so focused that we can't see what God places in front of us? Do we listen when He speaks? Sometimes, I believe, He sends angels in the form of people to guide us or to comfort us. Better still, I believe, He may send you or me to guide someone else. How many times has He saved your life? Do we get angry at others before we know the whole story? We may not have the vision to see what's ahead of us, but we should trust God to lead us. His path is to His kingdom.

(Num. 22:20, Num. 22:21–35)

Backfire

"Did I not send you an urgent summons to come to me?
Why did it take you all this time to saddle your donkey?
Am I not really able to reward you?
Don't you know all the things I can do?"
These are the words from Balak's mouth to Balaam's ears.
Balaam said, "Well I have come to you now. Have no fears.
Balak, you have summoned me. What must I do?"
"The words I speak will be God's words that are true.
Now build here on this site seven altars each.
Perhaps the Lord will reveal to me, if He decides to meet."
On each altar, Balaam and Balak offered a ram and a bull.
God spoke to Balaam about His message, and he understood.
"Come," he said, "curse Jacob for me."
"Come," he said, "and denounce Israel for me."
Balaam said, "I see a people who live apart.
I cannot curse a people close to God's heart."
"I will tell you again if you have any doubt.
I will only speak what the Lord puts in my mouth."
Balak said, "Come to another place to curse them for me."
Again a bull and ram were sacrificed on seven altars each.
Balaam met with God again to hear the words of the wise.
Balaam told Balak, "God is not human that He should lie.
Listen, Balak, to what the Lord God has to say.
They are like lioness that doesn't rest till it devours its prey.
The Lord God is with them.
The shout of the king is among them.
God is not a human being that He should change His mind.
Balak, I said I would speak His words. This is the third time."
Balak took Balaam to another place overlooking the wasteland,
Asking Balaam to curse the Israelites using God's hands.
Balaam said, "Build seven altars for the Lord's sacrifice,
Observing the Israelites camp set up tribe by tribe.

The prophecy of the one whose eyes sees clearly,

Prophecy of the one who sees a vision from the Almighty.

Be cursed those who may curse you.

Be blessed those who may bless you."

Balak said, "I summoned you to curse my enemies.

Now the Lord has kept you from being rewarded handsomely."

Balaam said, "I did tell you with all the palace's gold and silver

I would not take any but only give God's words to deliver.

Before I go home and go on my way,

Listen, Balak, to these warnings I need to say.

One who has knowledge from the Most High,

One who falls prostrate and who has open eyes.

A ruler from Jacob will come and destroy survivors of the city.

Edom and Seir will be conquered, the two of them his enemies.

Amalek was one of the first nations to begin.

Their utter destruction will become their end.

Listen, you Kenites, this message is the Lord's sixth.

You will be destroyed when Ashur takes you captive

Alas, who can live when this done from the God of the most?

Ships will come to the shores of Chittim coast.

They will come to ruin, but Ashur and Eber they will subdue.

Balak, I hope you have listened to the words God has told you.

From the very first message to God's very last,

All are from God and all will come to pass.

Balak, I have given God's words He told me to say.

I am returning home now, and I will be on my way."

Unless I am mistaken, God can use anyone He wants. In this case, He used Balaam to get His message across. Will you allow God to use you how He chooses? Will you answer the call when He does? Please find out who Balaam was.

(Num. 22:5–20, Num. 23:1, Num. 23:6–10, Num. 23:16–24, Num. 23:27–29, Num. 24:3–9 Num. 24:15–25, Num. 31:8, Num. 31:16, Rev 2:14)

Seduction and Destruction

When Moab started their seduction,

This also started their destruction.

Israel yoked itself to Baal, and the Lord's anger was ablaze.

He struck them with a plague, and 24,000 died during that day.

In Shittim, the men indulged in sex with the women of Midianite.

They bowed before their gods and ate their meals of pagan sacrifice.

The Lord God said to Moses, "If you want my anger to turn away,

Take the leader of these people; kill them, for all to see during the day."

Moses said to the judges of Israel's people,

"Each of you put to death those who have done evil."

At the tent of meeting, the entire assembly started to weep and cry.

An Israelite man brought a Midianitish woman to camp before Moses's eyes.

Phinehas, son of Eleazar, saw this and in his hand took a spear.

He knew what he had to do; he showed no fear.

God's anger was ablaze, and he knew Israel's fate was condemned.

Phinehas followed the couple and drove the spear into both of them.

The plague stopped, but 24,000 that day died.

The Lord said, "Phinehas has favor in my eyes.

He was zealous for God's honor and made atonement.

I put an end to my anger because of his commitment."

The Lord said to Moses, "Phinehas, grandson of Aaron the priest.

Tell Phinehas I am making a covenant with him of lasting peace.

This plague was a result for you being deceived.

The Midianites, kill them all. Treat them as your enemies.

Gather one thousand men from all twelve tribes.

Kill every man; leave none alive.

Kill all the boys and every woman who has slept with a man.

These are the ones that followed the advice of Balaam's plan."

God said, "Moses, you, Eleazar, and the heads of the community

Divide the spoils of war between all the soldiers equally."

The community, soldiers, and priest all got a share to keep all at ease.

All gave to the Lord's share, and the Lord God was pleased.

Why do we sin? I think for two reasons: it's fun and easy. Another tale of not believing in God after all He's done, reverting back to old habits. Sex is one of the oldest forms of straying from God. We all hear of the top three "money, sex, and violence." It seems not much has changed since the Israelites' time to present. What are your top three? Can you be stronger than them? The reoccurring theme is trust God and let Him lead.

(Num. 25:1–2, Num. 25:4–9, Num. 25:11–13, Num. 25:16–18, Num. 26 (second census), Num. 31:1–7, Num. 31:15–17, Num. 31:28–31, Num. 31:47–54, Rev. 2:14)

I truly hope you enjoyed read the book of Numbers as well as the poems. Numbers is a book of God's patience and mercy. How many times was He ready to strike down the Israelites? With Moses's prayers, He decided against wiping them out. A journey that should have taken only days or weeks took forty years to accomplish. What's the theme? Trust God! Because they didn't have faith and trust, God decided to allow the current generation to die and move forward with the next generation. Keep in mind Moses, Aaron, and Mariam were not exempt from the old guard and paid the consequences of their mistakes. None of them made it to the promised land. Moses was allowed to see it but not to enter. How will we pay for our mistakes? Will we enter the promised land?

Another significant story of the Bible is that of Balaam. In the coming book of Deuteronomy, this is what the Lord says of it in Deut. 18:10–12. Also, we have not made it to the New Testament, but in Gal. 5:19–21, was Balaam the pagan Moses? Whoever Balaam was, God used him as He wanted. Balaam delivered seven prophetic messages to the king of Moab of blessings, not curses, as he was instructed to do. How incredible God is. We need to understand this about God. No matter what and who we think we are, God can use us to give His message to anyone at any time. Have a Bible you understand and keep reading. Four pages per day and you will have the Bible read in one year. Please continue to read God's words and let His spirit fill you with the love of Him and others.

Poems

The following poems are about us. These pieces are *my* interpretations only, but they have biblical themes.

Shhh (God's Silence)

What do you do when God is silent?
When the demons are whispering in your ears,
What do you do when God is silent?
When the devil is giving you reason to have fear,
What do you do when you no longer hear God's voice?
Put your head in your hands, not knowing what to do.
What do you do when the devil offers a different choice?
Do you tighten your belt and lace up your shoes?
Do you think you are the only one to have doubt?
Just open God's book, and you will read that is not true
Moses thought he would fumble the words from his mouth,
But God sent Aaron with him, and his faith was renewed.
Moses said, "I am not the man to deliver your people."
What do you do when God listens to you?
Moses said, "I am not he to break their bondage from evil."
What do you do when God lets you do what you do?
What about David when he had to run from Saul the king?
What do you do when God sends you on your journey?
David was on his own, thinking God hadn't done one thing.
What do you do when you feel God isn't with thee?
This is what we read of David's tale from the start.
What do you do when you can't see the finish line?
But God said David was a man after his own heart.
By keeping faith, God rescues us each and every time.
What about John the Baptist, Jesus's cousin and kin?
What do you do when God gives you an unbelievable task?
John foretold the Savior that would come to die for our sins.
He gave us a message for all time that forever lasts.
John was spreading the word about Jesus, the only one.
What do you do when you feel isolated and alone?
John was speaking of salvation and to see God's kingdom
Because in the end, God will call us all home.

Perhaps God says this when He is silent:

"Use this quiet time for understanding and to repent.

I didn't send you alone on your journey.

You are not alone because I'm always with thee.

I know sometimes your mind has doubt.

I placed in your heart what I'm all about.

I know the devil is whispering in your ears,

But keep the faith and I will remove all fears.

I know this journey you could not see the end.

When I bring you home is when your journey begins.

Maybe sometimes my words are too loud and deafening.

Maybe sometimes my words are too soft because I'm whispering.

Maybe the other words you are hearing are too confusing?

Maybe you cut me off and you're not listening."

What do you do when God is silent?

What do we do when God doesn't answer right away? Do we blame Him? Do we curse Him? This piece speaks on a few that had the same doubts as us, and look how they were blessed! I think patience is the key and faith in God. What can't God do? Perhaps we miss the answer He sends because we are too busy with our lives. Sometimes we need to pay attention to the signs He sends and act on them.

Here is an example. If you want to cross the water to reach the other side, and you can't swim. A log floats by; you don't use it. An empty raft drifts by; you don't use it. A person comes next to you, jumps in, and swims across. You don't ask them to help you. Next, you blame God because He didn't get you across after you prayed endlessly. Here's what I think God would say. "I sent you a log, a raft, and a person, but you didn't listen to my answer." Sometime we think God is a babysitter for us or we are too prideful to take a lesser means. Do you not think our faith will be tested? Here's a word: humility.

Mighty Is It

It can spit venom
With the right words.
It can kill or destroy
Written correctly.
Nations can crumble.
People imprisoned
Harshly.
Women's esteem crushed.
Children afraid.
Men humbled.
More powerful than forged weapons.
Mightier than the sword.
With the spirit
Brings love,
Overwhelming joy,
Infectious smiles and laughter.
Invokes confidence.
Unites nations.
Destroys hate.
Truth about God
Lifts Jesus,
Invites the Holy Spirit.
What is it?
The Bible calls it the
Tongue.

The words we speak can kill a person. We can demean a person till eventually they commit suicide or homicide. Our words can destroy a person's self-esteem and even cause fear and panic in a crowd of people. Say the words "fire," "highjack," or "gun," and people will run to seek shelter. Now say the words "worthless," "ugly," or "nothing" to a person. What do you think their minds and hearts did? Probably sank. Once we utter some cruel words, we can't take them back because they have left our mouths. We can apologize, but the damage is done. We have been taught to think before we speak. How true. Our tongue is very powerful. When we use it to uplift each other, faces light up. Give someone a compliment today and every day. It will brighten their spirits. You never know; you could have saved a life just with your tongue!

Two Commandments

The two most important commandments Jesus degreed

Was for me to love God with everything I have in me

And for me to love my neighbor as I would love me.

And God will bless me abundantly

And give me all I need spiritually,

And the power of forgiveness will come naturally.

Jesus said, "All you have to do is to believe in me.

Just open your heart and follow faithfully.

Then you can command mountains to move and walk on seas."

This is what the power of prayer can do for me.

God's store of prayer is open for free.

Just walk in and take His blessings for free.

There are no tricks, nothing up His sleeve.

At his store there isn't a Help Wanted sign.

I'm called first to the front of the line.

In His store, He gives His advice for free,

And these are the things He says to me.

First of all, He says that He loves me.

And because of His Son's love, He forgives me.

Next He says to "Open your heart and follow me,

And I will bless you. Just wait patiently."

This is what the power of prayer can do for me.

The power of prayer opens my mind and gives clarity.

Let me break it down for those who don't believe.

No matter how much the devil tempts me,

I can ignore all he has because of God's Spirit in me.

And if I do all that He asks of me,

He keeps His promise, and His kingdom I will see.

He will give me more than my eyes can see.

Just remember these two commandments I will repeat,

For me to love God with everything I have in me

And for me to love my neighbor as I would love me.

If I do all of this, my soul will be complete.

I do this because His kingdom I want to see.

This is what the power of prayer can do for me.

How powerful are these two commandments? We should focus on what we can do rather than what we should not do. Remember, love God with all of your heart. For some this is difficult because we put money, cars, clothes, and sex before God. We also have hatred toward our neighbors, sometimes for the smallest of reasons. Please understand your neighbor can be a wife, husband, friend, or anyone. *There is a scripture, and I challenge you to look it up.* I will paraphrase; how can you love God, who you cannot see, and hate your brother that you see daily?

We sometimes don't like a person because of the shoes she wears, the way someone talks, how much or lack of education a person has. Once again, I am equally guilty, but we should strive to change our thinking. This is what the power of prayer can do for us! God created our minds and bodies to overcome a great many obstacles if we trust God. Think about this. When you truly want something, whether it is to stop smoking, get a degree or a new pair of shoes, when you set your mind and heart to it, what happens? It gets done. What is the difference in setting your mind and heart on God? If we truly want His blessings … think about it.

He's Coming

With God, you need a connection.

Keep your spirit open without objection.

You can start with your own reflection.

Look at your life and begin dissection.

Open your heart and let Jesus in,

And during this time, the Lord will come again.

Let the trumpets sound through thunder and rain.

He will come in His Father's name.

He will come like a thief in the night.

He will come for those whose souls are right.

The mountains will shake.

The earth will quake.

There will be hurricane winds.

Ocean's tide will be at an end.

All of nature will stand and cheer,

"The King of Host is near!"

Do not hide, do not turn away.

Jesus is here for those wanting to be saved.

Sing together without any fear,

"My Lord and Savior is here!

My beloved Jesus has come to take us home.

He has come to take us to the kingdom.

Those are not clouds but angel wings

Coming with Jesus, coming down with the King."

Not a deaf ear or a blind eye

When the Father comes again a second time.

You have been given time to get ready.

You have been given time to get steady.

The Father is coming.

The Father is coming.

Can't you feel it in your soul?

Can't you feel it from your head to your toes?

Your heart is racing with excitement.
Your face shines with enlightenment.
The saints can feel His Holy Spirit.
The saints are ready for a heavenly lift.
He's coming, my Jesus.
He's coming, my Savior.
He's coming, my Creator.
He's coming, my Healer.
He's coming, my Deliverer.
My Jesus is coming.
My Jesus is coming.
Thank God Almighty.
My Lord is coming.
Stand and shout, "My Jesus is coming!
The Lord of Host is coming!
Amen."

NCE, ESS, and ISS

What is kindness?

Is it something to dismiss?

Some call it graciousness

Because your heart has fullness.

Others may say sweetness,

To show your tenderness.

How about the term unselfishness?

Giving to others, showing thoughtfulness

Or a good neighbor helpfulness.

Taking time with their patience.

Even to rude people to have a tolerance.

Some even think it's a weakness,

Those in power showing benevolence,

Displaying all of their goodness.

I hope this poem brings feeling of pleasantness.

For me, it is just my friendliness.

Flesh

Kind Father,
I feel temptation of the flesh.
I know I'm weak.
It entices me.
It calls to me.
It wants me.
And I, it.
I lust for it.
Sometimes I crave it.
I know it's wrong,
But I enjoy it.
Times I can't get enough of it.
Now, I call upon you.
I need your strength.
Place your armor on me:
The belt of truth,
The breastplate of righteousness,
Feet with the gospel of peace,
The shield of faith,
The helmet of salvation,
The sword of the Spirit.
Then let me stand firm.
Let me stand strong.
Let me stand ready.
Keep my eyes fixed on you,
My mind sharp on heaven's high,
And my heart with Jesus.
Amen.

Deuteronomy

King

What is a king?

A king is many things.

A king is God appointed.

A king is God anointed.

A king won't take you back were you were oppressed

But builds on the land that God gives you to possess.

A king should know when to stay and when to fight.

A king should be one of your fellow Israelites.

He shouldn't return to the land of enslavement for horses and gold,

Nor to accumulate large amounts of silver and many wives for his fold.

Neither should he consider himself better and turn from the law.

All of this will be his undoing; this is his fatal flaw.

He is to write the law on a scroll taken from the Levitical priest,

To be with him to read all the days of his life to revere and teach.

If a king takes many wives, his heart will be led astray,

But following God's degrees, then he and his descendants will reign many days.

Coming from Egypt, all the Israelites knew, was having a king (Pharaoh) rule them. Having Moses in charge, was that not good enough? Is this one of the Israelites' fatal flaws, not letting God be in control? Is it ours? Why put our own mix into things? Who and what God does, is that not good enough? This will play a significant part with Israel in the coming chapters, especially in the book of Samuel. A prelude to Saul.

(Deut. 17:14–21)

Purge

"You must purge the evil from among you
To prevent your hearts from being evil seduced.
By sword or stone, show no pity; put them to death.
Purge this evil, follow my decrees, and you will be blessed.
If a prophet announces a wonder, and it comes true,
And says, 'Let's follow a god not known to you,'
Even if your family tries to turn you from me,
Or if troublemakers arise in the land I give to thee,
It is a test to whether or not you give your heart to me.
You must inquire; you must probe and investigate it thoroughly.
If found to be true, these detestable things being done among you.
This is my decree to follow that I am giving to you.
That prophet that tried to turn you away from me,
Put him to death for all of Israel to see.
Your family that tried to stop you from being blessed,
Do not spare them or show pity; stone them to death.
The troublemakers that want to take you from the Lord,
Burn the town and put the troublemakers to the sword.
Let all of Israel open their eyes and ears,
Let all of Israel think of evil and have fear.
Do not sacrifice an ox or sheep with a defect or flaw.
This is detestable to God; this is His law.
Anyone in violation of worshipping the sun, moon, or stars in the sky,
They are in violation of God's covenant, and you must take their life.
If found true by multiple testimonies of this evil deed,
Stone them to death at the gates of your cities.
The first to throw the stone must be from the witness's hands.
Next from all the people to purge the evil from the lands.
When judging cases, do not turn to the left or right.
Judge all cases fairly in the presence of God's sight.
Whether bloodshed, lawsuits, or assault,
Act accordingly, no matter who is at fault.

Those showing contempt for priests or judges ministering the Word,

Put them to death because evil from the lands must be purged.

When entering the land I'm giving you to possess,

Do not imitate their ways; you must be blameless.

Do not cast spells, do sorcery, consult the dead, or engage in witchcraft.

They sacrifice their sons and daughter; this is a detestable practice

There is no place in this land for any type of occult.

These nations land you will dispossess is their only result.

I will drive these nations out before you.

This is the covenant that I will keep to you.

Those false prophets who claim to speak in my voice.

I will raise a prophet from among you, which is my choice.

Anyone who hates thy neighbor and strikes him mortally

And flees to one of the three refuge cities,

The elder must hand him over to the avenger of blood to die.

Purge the guilt of innocent blood so all may be set right.

If parents have a son that doesn't heed their voice,

Take him to the elders of the town. This is God's choice.

Tell them he is rebellious, a glutton and a drunkard in your home.

Then all the men of the city shall put him to death by stones.

If a man rapes a virgin pledged to another man,

Put him to death. Purge this evil from the land.

Do nothing to the woman, no sin committed deserving of death.

But the man committed a sin deserving of taking his last breath.

If a man is found sleeping with another man's wife,

Both the man and woman will surely die.

You must follow my words, my laws, and my decrees.

Your Lord God detests these things and those who deal dishonestly.

You are my treasured people and keep my commands.

I will set you in praise above all nations in the lands.

Purge this evil.

You are my chosen people.

What I offer is not beyond your reach.

It is not in heaven or beyond the sea.

Do not ask who will cross the sea or ascend to heaven to get it.

The Word is very near you, in your mouth and heart so you may obey it.

Heaven and earth are witnesses to life, death, blessing, and a curse. Purge this evil, hold fast to me, because I put you as my people first."

How can the nation be holy, living with and in sin? How much sin do you live with? Do you call yourself a Christian? How much evil do you need to purge from your life? God wanted to make a point to His family that evil living and practices would not be tolerated. God did not want the Israelites to fall prey as other nations around them to pagan worship, and all evil must be purged. In this day and age, I don't think death is the answer to purging evil but by strong prayer and faith. With faith, God will give you the answer you need to purge yourself from whatever evils confront you. Unceasing prayer and unyielding faith in God, you can accomplish all.

(Deut. 13:1–18, Deut. 17:1–7, Deut. 17:8–13, Deut. 18:9–22, Deut. 19:11–13, Deut. 21:18–21, Deut. 22:22–27, Deut. 26:16–19, Deut. 30:11–20)

The book of Deuteronomy is a book to rededicate their lives to God. God will not tolerate sin with His holy people. With the new generation entering into the promised land, He is informing His people of the consequences of disobedience. Moses gave the Israelites a history lesson and restated the covenant. This is also the book where Moses dies. A very powerful message about purging evil from their lives.

We need to rededicate our lives to God and purge sin from our lives. How many of us look at our own lives and realize we need to purge? Is it a bad habit, words and thoughts? We all need to purge something. The poem "King" is a prelude to coming chapters of God's words. A period of time when the Israelites wanted a king to lead them instead of trusting God to continue to lead. After this group of poems, we dive headfirst into the book of Joshua. We should go to church for spiritual guidance and sanctuary for our souls. Do we go to His temple and disrespect His church?

There arise so much positive Godly spirit filling His temples. The joy of being with others like you to lift the name of Jesus and let that absorb into your entire being. The joy of song, prayer, music, study, honor, and saving souls. What a joy and pleasure to serve God. Unfortunately, many sins happen in churches; it is up to us to police ourselves to keep His temples sacred.

Poems

Joy in Heaven

Today, right before my eyes,

I witnessed someone being baptized,

And joy filled the entire church.

We all knew what it is worth.

With smiles on all faces, we knew this,

In the name of the Father, the Son, and Holy Spirit.

Baptism is an outward sign of commitment.

Inwardly your soul is ready, and you repented.

What joy it is giving your soul to God's Son,

Making a choice to journey to God's kingdom.

If you listen and concentrate on becoming a new being,

The heavens will open, and you can hear the angels singing.

Consumption

How can we love God, who we cannot see,

But hate our brother that we see daily?

I hope this poem touches all I as speak,

But most of all this poem was meant for me.

It's a reminder of no matter what people do to me,

I should love them as I love me.

We always hear about making it to the heavenly gates,

But how can we, when within our hearts we have hate?

Set yourself free and learn to forgive,

Or keep your hate if that's how you want to live.

Is it that you can't forgive the shame?

Or you don't know whom to blame?

Then don't say you're a Christian in Jesus's name.

All the times you lift your voice in song,

But can't forgive those who've done you wrong,

Those who curse you,

Those who abuse you,

Those who test you,

Those who hurt you.

People say, "I can forgive, but I won't forget."

But will that lingering pain cause you deep regret?

The scriptures say to forgive seventy times seven.

Will your unforgiving heart stop you from going to heaven?

You should love your neighbor as you love yourself.

This is the beginning of the journey to heaven's wealth.

Understand the power of forgiveness and what's at stake.

Forgiveness in your heart can take you to heaven's gate.

No matter what atrocities people do to you,

Jesus says, "Forgive them, Father, they know not what they do."

When you were put on punishment, did you forgive your mother?

When you were teased endlessly, did you forgive your brother?

All the times of not being there, did you forgive your sister?

Do you tell her you that you love her because you miss her?

Do you let that anger consume your soul?

Do you let the rage hang on and not let go?

Do not let anger control your soul and mind?

Let the anger and rage go, and Jesus you will find.

I'm sorry, I apologize are powerful words coming from the heart.

Between two people wronging each other, they can have a fresh start.

If you want to have that heavenly glow,

Forgive them because God said so.

If you want to live in heavenly bliss,

Practice forgiving, and His kingdom you can't miss.

Mother's Prayer

A mother's prayer is endless.
A mother's prayer is selfless,
Praying for her family unity,
Praying for her family's peace.
If you ever catch your mother on her knees,
Think, *Chances are, she is praying for me.*
If you ever noticed your mom with a huge smile,
She prayed for you; she prayed for her child.
She prays to keep you safe,
To keep you free from mistakes,
Praying to keep you injury-free,
To keep you happy and healthy.
Praying that when it's your time,
That you will keep God in your heart and mind.
Praying for the words when you speak
And God will watch over you when you sleep.
Now on your knees, every day you pray
For your children, now that you have raised,
Praying that they keep God near.
And all your prayers are sincere.
To know a mother's prayer, here's what you do.
Just ask. She will say, "I prayed for you.
I prayed for your life when you were born.
I prayed for a healthy daughter or son.
I prayed endlessly, and you are the result.
I prayed that you grow into a fine adult.
I pray that you will pray over your seed.
And God will give them all that they need."

Tithing

Tithing is a privilege,

So read and understand this.

Remember the job that you go to.

You are giving back what God gave to you.

Some people say, "I have to pay my tithes like a chore."

Take it as a blessing and give back what He asks for.

Be a cheerful giver from your heart.

Always know it is never too late to start.

God knows what you can give.

He knows the problems in your life you live.

He is the one that gives the ability of wealth.

He knows the hand you were dealt.

Remember to place Him first,

And not a day in your life will you thirst.

Please honor God with His tithes,

And He will bless you all the days of your life.

Joshua

The book of Joshua is the passing of the torch from Moses to his successor, Joshua. Joshua became an excellent leader of the Israelites. We need to remember that in order to lead, we must be a follower. Joshua had a great teacher in Moses and God. Are you a leader or follower? Or both? Of the old generation God promised the Israelites would not enter the promised land. None of the first generation alive except Caleb and Joshua because of their faith. This book is basically two parts; the first is the fight of conquest, and the second is the dividing of the land between the twelve tribes. Joshua, being an excellent military leader, engages in many battles to conquer the promised land. Please read about the triumph, failures, and struggles facing Joshua and the Israelites. Do the Israelites repeat the same mistakes as the last generation? The second part is the dividing of the promised land among the twelve tribes. Because lots were drawn, the twelve tribes knew which piece of land they were receiving. Driving out the remaining inhabitants proved more difficult for the Israelites, which also became a thorn in their side later. Keep reading, keep praying, keep the faith, and most of all enjoy God's words.

Twelve Stones and a Prostitute

Moses has died, and Joshua is now in charge of the twelve tribes.

To look over the land of Jericho, Joshua secretly sent out two spies.

They went about their journey and task but didn't know for how long.

When they entered Jericho, they stayed in a prostitute's home.

The prostitute Rahab's home was built into the walls of Jericho.

It was easy for strangers to come and easy for strangers to go.

And the king heard that spies had entered Rahab's home.

He ordered Rahab to send them out, fearing they threatened his throne.

She said, "They were here but left when the city gate was closed.

If you hurry, you can catch them out on the fords of Jordan Road."

But Rahab hid them on the roof away from prying eyes.

Later that night, she went up to talk to the two spies.

"We have heard of all of the wonders your God has done for you.

We are in fear, and our courage fails because of what your God can do.

What you did to Sihon and Og and dried up the water of the Red Sea.

Now swear to me by the Lord that you will show kindness to my family."

They replied, "Our lives for your lives if you don't tell anyone of our plans.

We will treat you kindly and faithfully when the Lord gives us the land."

She let them down by a cord and told them to hide in the hillside for three days.

They hid themselves from the king's pursuers and then went about their way.

When they met Joshua, they told him everything from start to finish.

"They are in fear of us, and the land is ours as God promised, as His gift."

Joshua rose early in the morning, and Israel set out for the Jordan River.

And Joshua said to the people to be ready because many wonders God would deliver.

God said to Joshua, "On this day, I will begin to exalt you for Israel to see.

I will part the Jordan River for you just as I did the Red Sea."

Joshua said to the people, "Consecrate yourselves. God will do wonders among you."

Then Joshua gathered the priest and told them what God wanted them to do

Before all the people passed by the Holy ark.

"This way you will know where to go before you depart.

Those who bear the covenant, you shall command the priest.

Waters from upstream of the Jordan shall stand in a heap."

The priest stood on dry ground in the Jordan from the water flow,

And all the nation finished passing over the Jordan opposite of Jericho.

God said, "Take twelve men to gather twelve stones where the priest stood firmly.

Where you lodge tonight, place them as a reminder of what I have done for thee.

Each man from each tribe, place it on his shoulder that it may be a sign,

And when your children ask about them, it will be a reminder for all time."

On that day in front of all Israel, God exalted Joshua in plain sight,

Just as they had stood in awe of Moses all the days of his life.

When the priests' feet were on dry ground, the Jordan waters began to flow.

The people came up out of the Jordan, camped at Gilgal east of Jericho.

The twelve stones they took out of the Jordan, Joshua set up in Gilgal's lands.

All the people of the earth would fear the might of the Lord God's hands.

The kings of the Amorites and Canaanites heard of God's work on the Jordan banks.

There was no longer any spirit in them to fight, and their hearts completely sank.

At that time, the Lord told Joshua to make flint knives to circumcise the people.

"The old generation all the men of war have died that I have rescued from Egypt was evil.

All the men of war wandering for forty years that did not obey me.

The ones I promised would perish and not see the land of milk and honey."

Joshua circumcised this nation as God commanded him to do.

The Lord God said, "I have rolled away the reproach of Egypt from you."

While camped at Gilgal, the people celebrated Passover on the Jericho plains.

They ate produce from the land, manna ceased, and they praised God's name.

By Jericho, Joshua lifted his eyes, and a man stood with a drawn sword in his hands.

Joshua said, "Friend or foe, because our Lord God has given us these promised lands."

The man said, "I am the commander of God's army. Now I have come."

Joshua fell facedown and worshipped, preparing for what must be done.

The commander said, "Take your sandals from your feet,

For the place where you are standing, this ground is holy."

The Lord said, "I have given you Jericho, king and all of its mighty men.

Because of the people of Israel, none may leave and none may go in.

You shall march around the city, all the men of war, for six days.

They will pass before the ark, and not one sound shall be made.

On the seventh day, seven priests with the rams' horns will make a long blast.

Then all the people will shout greatly, and the walls will fall down flat."

Joshua commanded the people, priests, and the army to march around the city.

They obeyed and marched with the Ark of the Covenant six days silently.

Only the priest bearing the seven trumpets of rams' horns blew continually.

All of Jericho was doomed except Rahab the prostitute and her family.

She and her family were safe because she hid the two spies entering Jericho.

The symbol of her safety was a scarlet cord she bound in her window.

Now it came to pass on day seven when Israel rose about the dawning of the day.

Israel marched around the city six times, as they had done the other six the same way.

On the seventh time around, the rams' horns were blown by the priest.

Joshua said to the people, "Now shout, for the Lord's destruction is unleashed."

The people let out a great shout, and the walls fell down flat of the city.

The army entered. All was destroyed by the army's sword showing no pity.

"Man and woman, young and old, ox, sheep, and donkey,

Take what belongs to the Lord and set fire to the city."

Joshua charged them by this curse: "The man that builds this city, this is his fate.

He shall lay its foundation with his firstborn and his youngest set its gate."

Because of his faith, on Joshua, God placed his hands.

The Lord was with him, and Joshua's reputation grew throughout the lands.

A prostitute! Really! Yes, a prostitute, because our God can use anyone He wants to accomplish anything He wants. Will you let Him use you? Will you open yourself to Him to be used? We may think God uses someone who is not worthy. Remember Balaam? What is the significance of the twelve stones? Were the stones a reminder or to keep Israel focused on what He had done for them? What is in your life that reminds you of God's work with you? We may not have a Jericho to conquer, but what walls do you need to fall in order to let Jesus in?

(Josh. 2:1–7, Josh. 2:8–13, Josh. 2:9–23, Josh. 3:1–8, Josh. 12–16, Josh. 3:17, Josh. 4:1–9, Josh. 4:10, Josh. 4:12–21, Josh. 5:1–9, Josh. 5:9–15, Josh. 6:1–7, Josh. 8–13, Josh. 6:15–23, Josh. 6:26–27)

Trader and a Spear

Joshua sent some men to spy out the next town in the east.

They reported back that it would take only a few thousand to defeat.

So approximately three thousand warriors were sent to capture the town.

Ai defeated the Israelites on the slopes, and they came running down.

Paralyzed with fear, the Israelites' courage melted away.

They threw dust on their heads, tore their clothes in dismay.

Joshua cried out, "Oh sovereign Lord, why did you bring us to this place?

Just to have our enemies hear of this, surrounds us, and wipe us from earth's place"

What will happen to the honor of your great name?"

The Lord said, "Get up because one of you has brought great shame.

One of you has stolen things I commanded to be set apart for me.

This is why Ai defeated you, because I was not with thee.

Among their belongings, they have lied, and they have hidden my things.

Unless they are destroyed, I am not with you, and destruction will it bring.

Get up and purify yourselves, for tomorrow, here is what you will do.

Morning, each tribe will come forward, and I will point them out to you.

Tribe by tribe and clan by clan,

One by one until remains the guilty man."

Morning, Joshua brought out the tribes until Judah remained.

From Carmi to Zerah until Achan, the man who brought the shame.

Joshua said, "Don't hide it from me, and tell the truth, my son."

Achan replied, "It's true, I've sinned, and a horrible thing I've done.

I saw a Babylon robe, two hundred silver coins and a bar of gold weighing more than a pound.

I have them, they are hidden beneath my tent, and I buried them deep in the ground."

They found the items and brought them before the Lord and all of Israel to see.

They took Achan, all he owned, his family, and took them to the Achor Valley.

All the Israelites stoned Achan and his family and burned the bodies.

They piled a heap of stones over Achan, so the Lord was no longer angry.

Then the Lord said to Joshua, "Don't be afraid or discouraged of one thing.

You will destroy them as you destroyed Jericho and its king."

Joshua chose thirty thousand of his best warriors and sent them out at night.

"Hide in ambush close behind the town, ready for action and ready to fight.

When our main army attacks, Ai's men will run out, and we will run away.

'Look—the Israelites are running from us, as before,' is what they'll say.

While we are running, jump from your ambush and take possession of the town.

For the Lord your God will give it to you then burn it to the ground."

Across the valley, the king of Ai saw the Israelites.

He and his men charged the Israelites ready to fight.

There was not a man left in Ai or bethel to defend.

The town was left open, and the five thousand ambushers just walked in.

God said, "Point your spear toward Ai. This is the signal to abide by.

You will quickly capture the town, set it on fire, and smoke will fill the sky."

When the men of Ai looked behind, surrounded with nowhere to turn,

With the Israelites on both sides, they were defeated as their town burned.

Only the king, being brought to Joshua, was taken alive.

The entire population of Ai of twelve thousand, no one survived.

"Burn the city; keep the treasure and the plunder as our own."

The king of Ai, Joshua hung and buried him with a heap of stones.

On Mt. Ebal, Joshua built an altar to the Lord Almighty,

Giving praises and presenting offerings for their recent victory.

With the priest in the middle, Joshua read to the people as Moses had done.

He read the blessings and curses Moses wrote in the book of instruction.

He read every word of every command, and he didn't add anything new.

The people stood in assembly, and the Lord's covenant was renewed.

Greed in earthly items have been our downfall for a very long time. Achan was no different, and he paid dearly for it. Remember the saying, what is in the dark will come to the light. If we are going to be greedy, then be greedy for God's Word, His love, His spirit but share it with others. What would you trade your life for? What riches of the earth are worth your life? The spear has very significant meaning, just the same as Moses's staff (Exod. 17:11). We must always listen and follow God's plan. Do you think He can go wrong? Make sure you have a Bible you understand and keep reading.

(Josh. 7:2–9, Josh. 7:10–15, Josh. 7:16–22, Josh. 7:24–26, Josh. 8:1–8, Josh. 8:14–17, Josh. 8:17–34)

Thirty-One Flavors

From Jericho to the king of Jerusalem,

All thirty-one kings fell under the Israelite's thumb.

Because of Joshua's faith in the King of Kings,

All fell, including the northern and southern kings.

All the kings west of the Jordan heard what Joshua had done,

Combining their armies to become united as one.

Now, the people of Gibeon resorted to deception and treachery.

They came bearing gifts to the camp of Israel for a peace treaty.

They put on worn clothes, old saddlebags, and patched wineskins.

Unknown to Joshua, they had a scheme behind those inviting grins.

Joshua said, "We don't know you. How can we make peace with you?"

They answered, "We come from afar. We are your yours. Tell us what to do.

Our elders and people instructed us to take supplies on this journey.

This bread was hot from the oven when we left; now it's dry and moldy.

From this long journey, our wineskin split open, and our sandals are worn.

Our donkeys are tired, and our clothes are ragged and torn.

We are your servants, and we have come to make the peace.

We've heard of what your God has done to the Amorite kings of the east."

But Joshua did not seek the Lord God's advice.

He made a treaty bound by oath with them by leaders of the Israelites.

Three days later, the Israelite learned they lived nearby.

Joshua called the men of Gibeon and asked, "Why did you lie?"

They said, "God told Moses to give you the land, and we feared you greatly.

Do to us whatever you think is right. We are at your mercy."

Joshua, a man of his word, honored the peace treaty.

He made them woodcutters and water carries to the Israel community.

When the king of Jerusalem heard of the treaty with the Gibeonites,

He sent word to other kings to join his army and ready themselves to fight.

They attacked Gibeon, all the Amorite kings from the hill country.

Gibeon sent word to Joshua. "Don't abandon your servants now," they pleaded.

Joshua, the entire army, and his best warriors traveled all night.

They defeated all the hillside armies of the invading Amorites.

God threw the Amorites in a panic, and many were killed by the sword

Retreating from Bethhoron, and the rest killed by hailstorm from the Lord.

In front of all Israel during victory, these are the words Joshua prayed.

"Let the sun stand still over Gibeon, the valley of Ajalon. Let the moon stay."

The sun stood still, and moon stayed until Israel defeated its enemies.

Joshua and the army continued the slaughter and wiped out the five armies,

But the five kings escaped and hid themselves in a cave.

Joshua had the cave covered. "It will be their grave."

Joshua left guards so the kings couldn't escape or be set free,

Then chased all that remained until they entered the fortified cities.

At the camp of Makkedah, the Israelites returned to Joshua safely.

Afterward, Joshua said, "Remove the rocks and bring the five kings to me.

Before I strike them down and put them to death,

Commanders, come forward and put your feet on their neck.

Don't be afraid. This is what your Lord will do to whom all you fight.

They will fear us because of the power of the Lord's might,

From town to town, village to village, destroying all in the lands,

Leaving no survivors, just as the Lord God of Israel commands."

In a single campaign, all the southern kings were laid to waste,

The hill country, the foothills and mountain slopes, leaving none in his wake.

The king of Jabin heard and sent word from the foothills to the slopes,

Seeking help to battle the Israelites in a desperate attempt of hope.

All the kings came, and their combined armies formed a vast horde.

Their horses and chariots covered the landscape like sand on the seashore.

God said, "Come tomorrow. I will hand them to you. Don't be afraid of their forces.

They will be dead men. Afterward, burn all their chariots and cripple their horses."

Joshua did as commanded because he was honor bound.

They had victory; they plundered, took livestock, and ravaged the town.

Because of Joshua and his entire legion,

They conquered the entire region,

From the Amorites to the Canaanites,

From the Hivites to the Jebusites,

From the hill country to the mountain slopes,

From Jerusalem to the king of Jericho.

By faith in God, Joshua did as commanded, and his faith did not waver.

A total of thirty-one kings defeated, hence the title: "Thirty-One Flavors."

The fighting to conquer the promised land could have been easier if the Israelites kept faith in God. The Israelites did not drive out all the inhabitants from the land, and that proved to be a mistake later. Thirty-one kings were defeated, and the land was divided among the twelve tribes. Joshua renewed the covenant and died at the age of 110. Only he and Caleb were allowed into the promised land of the latter generation. How much fighting would you do to enter the promised land? Will your faith be as strong as Joshua's? We should be careful of people bearing gifts with ulterior motives, sheep in wolves' clothing. Will we be as quick to fall prey to deception? That is the primary reason we need to seek God's counsel first, to ask Him for advice in all matters.

(Josh. 9:1–8, Josh. 9:11–27, Josh. 10:1–5, Josh. 10:6–11, Josh. 10:12–15, Josh. 10:16–27, Josh. 10:40–42, Josh. 11:1–3, Josh. 11:4–15, Josh. 12)

This is the end of the book of Joshua poems, and I hope you enjoyed the pieces. We move on to the book of Judges, another period in the Israelites' lives when they needed someone to lead them back to God. Before we start the book of Judges, let's talk about the devil and his quest to be number one in all of heaven, earth, and the entire universe. Remember the theme, four pages per day and a Bible translation that you can understand. Keep reading!

Satan, the Devil, Lucifer

How can we speak on Jesus without speaking on Lucifer? Remember, he is active and part of our lives; how much depends on your faith, your love for God, and your convictions. Do I have to remind you of the Israelites? How many times did they put God second and fall back into sin? Some of these pieces are written in the first person, as if I were Satan himself, speaking about how he would feel. His testimony. Keep in mind, Satan is a liar, which means these poems may twist the truth, but it's up to you to determine that.

The next pieces are my spin on the devil. Of course being boastful and arrogant, thinking I'm the *man* but at the same time conceding to Jesus. These poems also speak on what we should and should not do if we want to make it to the kingdom. Remember it's *my* interpretation and *my* spin on the subject. These are just a reminder that Satan is alive and active. Stay faithful to Jesus! Have fun reading.

I'm a Bad Man

I am Satan, the devil, and I'm bad to the bone.

I'm so bad I tried to take over God's throne.

Just listen to my personal testimony.

I took a third of God's angels down with me.

Remember my wings covered the throne for all angels to see

And my voice was one that all the angels envied.

I'm so bad, three times I tempted God's Son.

I do stuff like that just for fun.

Remember the original sin wasn't Cain and Abel or Adam and Eve.

It was me committing the first sin of having jealousy.

Remember I am the king ... of lies.

My henchmen are always standing by your side,

Ready to spread lies and ready to spread gossip,

Knowing with the right words your faith will soon slip,

Knowing you don't study the Word as you ought to.

I mix truth with lies and let you do what you do.

I know forgiveness isn't in your heart

Because you didn't like them from the very start.

Because of the sins I told you to do,

Your life span was a few hundred, now it's only a few.

I'm so bad I can have you hate your neighbor like no other.

I'm so bad I had Cain kill his brother.

So you think you can truly try to fight me.

How can you when you don't read the Bible daily?

So let me get this straight.

We started with ten, now we got eight.

My bad, we actually got only six or seven.

I took care of about three of them before I left heaven.

I think all ten were broken before they got to the promised land.

So who do you think got the upper hand?

I was just getting started, so who do you think will win?

This is my craft. I am the originator and mastermind of sin.

Those scriptures in Exodus just slipped your mind.

Now it started at ten and just went to nine,

What happened to the Ten Commandments God gave you?

Just in this poem I reduced them to only a few.

How can you go toe to toe with me and think you can win?

Before God created you, I was inventing new ways to sin.

Maybe if you had listened to God from the very start

By obeying Him and keeping the Holy Spirit in your heart.

Perhaps if you do what He asks of you every day,

Read the Bible daily and never forget to pray.

Maybe you need to have the power of forgiveness from the start

And love God with all that you have in your heart.

Maybe you will have your armor on when I come to tempt thee.

Until then, you don't want to mess with me!

Lucifer was around before God created humankind. The Bible tells us that there was war in heaven and Lucifer took one third of the angels with him. In my opinion, Lucifer had to have some juice! He had major influences on the heavenly angels to take as many as he did to convince them to go to war against God. That speaks volumes. That says much about Lucifer. Here are some words: vain, jealous, ambitious, narcissism, unhappy, domineering, impatient, leader, organizer, inspiration, and many more. In case you didn't notice, some words are interchangeable with positive thinking. But think about it, if he was all negative, would he have the following he did? Had to be a leader, yes. Had to be an organizer, yes. Had to inspire, yes. He had to be all of this in order to get angels to go against their Father God the Creator.

When God created man and woman, how long had Satan had practice in deception and lies? I am sure Satan knew that if he could deceive angels, surely humans would be easy targets. We were and are. It did not take much for Eve or Cain. How much does it take for you? A new car, purse, or person in your life? What is your trigger? Is it money, sex, drugs, or fame? Once you know what can tempt you, that's the very thing you need to pray for strength to avoid. Remember, Satan has had so much time to practice and perfect his craft.

We can't fight Satan physically, but with faith and prayer, we can keep temptation and sin to a low minimum. We all sin, and we all have temptation in our lives. How we deal with the two will definitely define who we are. It is difficult because sinning is easy and fun. It's the norm, but as Christians, we should want to be different. We should want to be an example from the norm. The really cool part is when you do what is right in God's eyes. Just be patient and watch what God does for you! His blessings are spectacular. Some of you know and have received His blessings and can testify to His love.

He Made Me Do It

I get blamed for everything.

It's all my fault, so it seems.

You didn't take care of your home; it was me.

You left Jesus alone; it was me.

You stole goods like a thief; it was me.

You told God you don't believe; it was me.

Every time something bad happens, it was me.

But God made you to have a choice that is free.

I was there when God made you. I know it's not me.

He gave you dominion first, but you still blame me.

All I am is a different choice.

All I am is a tiny voice.

Did I put the apple on Eve's table?

Did I kill Cain's brother Abel?

Did I actually commit these crimes?

Or was it already inside your mind?

Who was here first? Was it me or was it humankind?

It seems this has always slipped your mind.

But I made you do it.

Thou shall not steal.

You do it anyway, no big deal.

When you took God's name in vain,

Again it was me that took all the blame.

Is it me, that person you don't like?

It is me, for always starting office fights?

Is it me, for that neighbor you hate?

It is me, for you not wanting to pray?

I will take the blame from the very first day

As long as you own up for your lack of faith.

Thou shall not have any other Gods before me.

But you worship the moon, stars, and the green-back money.

I know, I made you do it.

But if you are listening to my voice,

That means you still have a choice.

To your father and mother you can give honor and respect,

You can work six days, and on the seventh you can give rest.

And I need to quit.

That's right, I made you do it.

Your choice is free,

But thank you for worshipping me.

I no longer recruit the way I used to.

You love sin. I let you do what you do.

Again, I know I made you do it.

People always say the devil is very busy.

Nope. I'm watching the show for free.

By the look on your faces, you are telling me to quit,

But I'm not the one that made you do it.

Your soul already has a For Sale sign on it.

You sin too much; you don't know when to quit.

You need to remember that I am heaven sent,

But I'm not the one stopping you to repent,

No matter how many stories people tell.

Don't forget I was created as an angel.

All I have discussed, did it happen during Adam and Eve?

Or is it something you can see on your flat-screen TV?

You value human's independency

Instead of God's dependency.

That's right, I took away your choice.

I made you listen to my voice.

But I'm not the only voice in your ear.

If you listen closely, God's words are very clear.

If you follow His guide,

He can give everlasting life,

If you let His spirit fill your heart,

You and God will never be apart.

Pick up the Word and follow Jesus's plan,

Guaranteed to make you a better human.

Let God in and He will remove the hate.

When He comes again to take you to the gates,

Just pray and have faith that God can get you through it.

If not, you can always say, "The devil made me do it."

How many of us are so quick to blame the devil for all the problems we go through? Especially the bad times, the hard times. But doesn't God allow us to go through troubled waters to strengthen us? How do we know which is which? Is it not true that God allows us to go through these hard times because He knows we will need to be stronger later? We may not fully understand why at the moment we are deep in it, but maybe years later, the lightbulb goes off, and we smile and thank Him. We say, "Thank you, Jesus." All adversity is not bad, and all waters are not troubled. As we move closer to the Father of heaven and earth, the more we can identify some of the reasons we have these hard times. Try to spin it into a positive. For example, we complain about bills. One, be blessed that you have a job to pay them, and the most important, God woke you up this morning, so it is an opportunity to change anything in your life. It is very important that we take responsibility for our actions. My last question: will you continue to say, "The devil made me do it"?

Nuthin' on Him

I'm the smoothest brother on the planet.

I got to be, because of all my gifts.

My tongue is the very best of them all.

My gift of tongue caused a third of the stars to fall.

I have you misquoting scriptures each and every day.

Is it in the Bible or is it something people like to say?

The lack of respect for your elders I cannot measure.

And the way you mistreat your parents gives you pleasure.

Sibling against sibling,

Fighting over petty things.

Mother against daughter and father against son.

Then you laugh about the things you've done.

Do you think I have horns and a tail?

I come as a person, a thing, or even an e-mail.

I come from all sides. I bring the heat and fire.

I know you all too well. I'll give you your desires.

So, if you keep being on my side,

You will forfeit your eternal life.

If you keep doing what I ask you to do,

You will miss His blessing He gives to you.

If you stop reading His words every day,

You won't know my lies with the words I say.

If you continue to stay on this path of sin,

Your soul will be mine, and I will win.

If you keep telling God you need a break,

How do you know which form I will take?

If you don't want to take a stand against sin,

Do you think you will meet Jesus in the end?

If you stop believing this huge lie,

That you are in control and let Jesus drive.

He will drive to the front of the pearly gates,

You will sing with angels, and His name you will praise.

And when you praise Him, you will come to appreciate
Why He died for you and why you pray in His namesake.
You pray with the Father in the beginning.
The prayer is His spirit, and His Son is the ending.
Like I said, I know I am so smooth.
But Jesus … I ain't got nuthin' on that dude!

What are the first words when you pray? Maybe *dear Father*, *heavenly Father*, or something to that degree. That's the Father in the beginning, and *my view* is the entire prayer is His Spirit entering you to pray for your blessings. Now, how do you end your prayer? Maybe in the name of Jesus or for the sake of Jesus, amen; this is the ending. Again my point of view.

Why do we think the devil looks like a beast? Is it the media or what we were taught? Lucifer was an angel. We were also taught that he had wings to cover the throne of God and a beautiful voice. Does this sound like a monster? The Word does say, "Behold and I saw a beast," but that's in Revelation (we will get there soon). The only way to recognize the *form* of the devil is the vigilant study of God's words. Of course, faithful prayer for wisdom and understanding of His words would be beneficial as well. We definitely need to remember Satan knows the Word better than we do, and he will twist lies and truth together. Will you know the truth when you hear it?

True Faith

If you fast for forty days, I don't think you could walk,

And without food or water, it would be difficult to talk.

Now here comes the one that was cast out.

The devil, Satan, or Lucifer, if you have any doubt.

God left him in the wilderness all alone.

I will show him a place that he can call home.

The devil said, "This is my moment to give all that I have.

I got the silky smooth tongue and the gift for gab.

My words are so smooth no one can resist me.

After all, I took a third of God's angels down with me.

Jesus, I remember everything that God has said.

But if you're the man, turn this stone into bread.

Jesus, I know you're weak, but I got you.

I know your strength is low, so I will carry you.

I will carry you to the holy city's highest spot.

Just jump from here; it's not a long drop.

Because if you are who you say you are,

God will send His angels to catch you from the stars."

Satan tried to tempt Jesus with his swag and his charm.

"Just jump, Jesus. Not a hair on your head will be harmed.

Let me carry you to the mountaintop to show all I have for thee.

Just remember I'm the man. Now bow down and praise me.

All of this is yours, everything that your eyes can see.

All you have to do is kneel down and worship me."

I will show him all my treasures and all of my gifts.

Jesus is weak, and he's tired, so I know he can't resist.

But Jesus told Satan, "I see through your lies.

My dear Satan, God has never left my side.

I know your words are twisted and full of deceit.

Very soon God will give me strength to stand on my feet.

Satan, God said from bread alone people do not live

But from every word of the scriptures that God gives.

I don't need to jump to know that I can fly

Because my wings are given to me by the Most High.

The scriptures say, 'Please don't put God to the test.'

My faith is in me, top of the line, the very best.

No, Satan, I will not bow and worship thee.

Look now, for my Father is sending angels to comfort me.

Get out of here, Satan. Get thee away from me.

My Father shows His love, and He is with me.

How can you offer what is not yours and what is not thine?

Don't you know, Satan? All that you offer is already mine?"

Does the word "persistent" mean anything? You have to admit, Satan is persistent to wanting to be in charge. He couldn't get it done in heaven, and now he's tempting Jesus, God's Son. Do we have the faith to resist temptation? Or would we give in to our hearts' desires? Will we join Lucifer in the last days in his plan to take over? Will our faith hold steadfast? Remember Satan knows the Bible better than we do. We need to be vigilant in studying of the Word. This is the only way to know truth from lies. Satan is a master of this, mixing lies with truth. We all must continue to pray for strength and study His Word, especially when we're weak.

Judges

The book of Judges explains exactly what the book is about, judging. The Israelite leader Joshua soon dies, and the Israelites go in a downward spiral toward evil. The first part of chapter 3 explains why Israel went through years of oppression. God left nations in Canaan to test the Israelites' faith to Him and to see if they would obey His commands. Each time a leader was not in place, the Israelites went back to pagan worship. Do you need someone to lead you? Will you allow God to lead?

Almost every period during the times of judging starts the same way: "Once again Israel did evil in the Lord's sight." But this also shows God's grace and mercy. We can always call upon the Lord for help, even after we sin. What a God, what a God. Come to the Father honest, humble, and truly seeking His mercy, and He will answer. Do you think, unlike the Israelites, you won't be put to the test of your faith? Patience, guidance, and wisdom are so important in our spiritual lives. As you read, you will learn that not all the tribes took control of the land given to them by God, or they had a very difficult time removing the inhabitants.

Judges gives one famous story we all know, the one about Samson and Delilah. Many other judges are not as famous but have significant meaning that can affect our lives today. To me, what is so amazing about the Bible is that the events that happened so many years ago are still true today. Keep reading His Word and enjoy.

A Judge, a Peg, and a Woman

After Judge Ehud died,

Israel did evil in the Lord's eyes.

The Lord sold them to Jabin into his hands.

Sisera the commander ruled with nine hundred chariots across the lands.

For twenty years he oppressed the people of Israel harshly.

Israel cried out to the Lord to deliver them from this cruelty.

Now, Deborah, a prophetess, the wife of Lapidoth, was judging at the time.

She sent and summoned Barak and said, "God has given me a sign.

God commands you to call out ten thousand warriors deep,

And God will call out Sisera, the commander of Jabin's army.

From the tribes of Zebulun and Naphtali will be your army."

Barak told her, "I will go but only if you go with me."

She replied, "Very well, but the honor will be by a woman's hands.

You will receive no honor when God conquers these lands."

Now, Sisera took nine hundred chariots and his warriors to the Kishon River.

He did not know victory was in a woman's hands to deliver.

Deborah said to Barak, "Get ready. God is marching ahead of you.

Victory is granted no matter what Sisera's warriors do."

When Barak attacked, God sent Sisera's army in a panic on the slopes.

Courage failed his armies; their fight left and removed all their hope.

Sisera leaped from his chariot, escaped, and took flight.

He ran into the tent of Jael, the wife of Heber the Kenite.

Because King Jabin and the Kenites' terms were friendly,

Sisera didn't think any of them would be his enemy.

Jael said, "Don't be afraid," and inside Sisera did go.

Sisera said, "If anyone asks if anyone is here, just say no."

Exhausted from all the fighting, Sisera fell asleep.

Jael took a hammer and tent peg and started to creep.

She crept up to Sisera without making a sound,

Driving the peg through his temple and into the ground.

When Barak came looking for Sisera his enemy,

Jael met him and said, "I will show you whom you seek."

Barak found Sisera dead on the ground before his eyes,

Victory by a woman, just as Deborah had prophesied.

On that day, Israel saw God defeat Jabin, and they became strong.

Israel finally defeated King Jabin, and Deborah and Barak sang a song.

"You who sit on fancy saddle blankets and who walk along the road,

Listen to the village musicians gathered at the watering holes.

Hooves hammered to the ground, galloping of Sisera's mighty steeds.

He sank, he fell, he lay still at her feet."

And for forty years the Israelites had peace.

They put their faith in God, and they believed.

Deborah was Israel's only woman judge and the fourth. During these times, it was unusual for a woman to lead, but then again, God chooses leaders by His standard, not ours. Will you let your gender hold you back? Your race or a disability? God sets the standards for those He wants to lead. Balaam, Rahab, and you. Judges, chapter 5, is the entire song of Deborah and Barak. I only inserted four lines from this beautiful song.

(Judg. 4:1–4, Judg. 4:6–10, Judg. 4:12–17, Judg. 4:22–23, Judg. 5:1–31)

A Fleece and the Three Hundred
Birth of a Hero—Part I

The Israelites did evil in the Lord's sight.

The Lord handed them over to the Midianites.

The Midianites were so cruel the Israelites hid in caves.

The Israelites lived in fear; none stood to be brave.

For seven years this oppression was done by the Lord.

The Midianites swarmed Israel like a locust horde.

They left Israel with nothing to eat,

Taking livestock, cattle, and their sheep.

Israel was reduced to the point of starvation.

They cried out to the Lord for His salvation.

God said, "I brought you up from all who oppressed you,

When will you realize there is nothing your Lord God cannot do?

I drove out your enemies and gave you their land.

This was not done by you but my own two hands.

But you have not listened to me.

This is why you don't live oppression-free."

The angel of the Lord came to Ophrah and sat beneath the great tree.

At this time, Gideon, son of Joash, was hiding while he was threshing wheat.

The angel appeared and said, "The Lord is with you, hero of might."

Gideon replied, "If true, why did you hand us over to the Midianites?"

The Lord said, "Go with your strength. Rescue Israel. I am sending you."

"But, God, my clan is the weakest. What can one man do?"

Gideon said, "Show me a sign that the Lord is speaking to me,

But don't go away until I come back with my offering to thee."

Gideon cooked a young goat and bread without yeast.

He presented them to the angel under the great tree.

"Place the meat and bread on this rock and pour the broth over it."

Fire shot up from the rock when the angel touched it with his staff's tip.

And then the angel disappeared.

Gideon cried out to the Lord in fear.

"I'm doomed. I have seen the angel of the Lord face-to-face."

"It's all right," replied God, "I will not wipe you from this place."

An altar called Jehovah-shalom was built in that place.

The altar remains in Ophrah, land of Abiezrites, to this day.

That day the Lord said, "Build an altar on the hilltop sanctuary.

Pull down your father's altar to Baal, laying the stones carefully.

Take a second bull from your father's herd that's seven years old.

As fuel for firewood for the burnt offering, cut down the Baal pole."

Taking ten servants, Gideon did as God commanded that night.

In the morning, people of the town arose and saw remains of the sacrifice.

For cutting down Baal's altar, the people wanted Gideon killed.

Joash shouted, "Why defend Baal if he is a god, who has the will?"

Soon after the armies of Midian and Amalekite formed an East alliance.

The Spirit of God took over Gideon. Now he is God's giant.

He blew the ram's horn, and many responded from different tribes,

A call to arms summoning God's warriors to stand at his side.

Gideon said to God, "If you want to use me, I need proof.

Tonight, I will place on the threshing floor a fleece of wool.

In the morning, if the ground is dry and the fleece is wet with dew,

Then I know you are God, and its Israel you command me to rescue."

In the morning, it was so as Gideon had asked.

"Don't be angry, Lord, but I have another task.

This time let the fleece be dry and the ground covered in dew."

Now it's done, and Gideon is ready for what God wants him to do.

God spoke and said, "You have too many warriors ready to fight.

If I let all fight, they will say it is not done by the Lord's might.

Tell the people, all that answered the call for Israel to be saved,

'You may go home, all that are timid and all that are afraid.'"

Twenty-two thousand warriors left, but the ten thousand remaining were too many to bring.

God told Gideon, "I will test them. Take them down to the spring.

Whoever drinks the water in a certain way,

This is the group for battle that will stay.

Those who drink from the stream as they kneel down,

Send them back to their families and back to their town.

The three hundred men that drink with their hands,

These are your warriors to take back the lands."

(Judg. 6:1–10, Judg. 6:11–19, Judg. 6:20–31, Judg. 6:33–39, Judg. 7:1–7)

I would like for you to think about this. The Midianites were so cruel that the Israelites had to hide in caves! Really think about that kind of cruelty, those kind of people. Unimaginable. Now think about this. We just finished the book of Joshua, and God gave the Israelites the land of milk and honey. Do you think they would be oppressed if they listened to God? Would they have to hide from anyone? We may not have someone oppressing us, but are you hiding? From what or whom? We have barely touched the Bible, and the reoccurring theme is to trust God first. We all fall short of His glory, but we should instinctively place God at the top of our go-to list for advice. It becomes easier the more we go to Him for all aspects of life. Whom do you go to first? Your friend, spouse, relative, or even your pastor?

A Fleece and the Three Hundred
Death of Gideon—Part II

The Midian army camp was in the valley below.

That night the Lord told Gideon to get up and go.

"I have given you victory, but if you still have doubt,

Take your servant Phurah to listen what they are all about."

Gideon listened to God and had courage to take the first step.

He overheard a man telling his dream in the enemy camp as he crept.

"A loaf of barley bread hit a tent and knocked it flat in my dream.

The Lord has given victory to Gideon, son of Joash, is what it means."

When Gideon heard this interpretation, he bowed and worshipped.

He divided the three hundred with a ram's horn, clay jar, and a torch in it.

"Keep your eyes on me. When I come to the edge of camp, do as I do.

As soon as I and those with me blow the ram's horn, blow yours too.

For the Lord and Gideon, shout as loud as you can,

Do this after midnight; changing the guard is their plan."

Suddenly they broke the clay jars and blew the rams' horns.

The Midianites rushed around in a panic and went into alarm.

Three hundred blew the horns, and the Midianites fought each other with the sword.

They were delivered to Gideon's hands, as prophesied by God the Lord.

Gideon sent word to cut them off in the shallows of the Jordan River,

Killing the two Midianites commanders by God's hands delivered.

The people of Ephraim asked Gideon, "Why do you treat us this way?

Why weren't we first to fight during the very first day?"

In heated words with Gideon, Ephraim stated their angry case.

Gideon said, "My clan's harvest is nothing compared to your leftover grapes."

When they heard his response, their anger subsided with ease.

Taking his three hundred across the Jordan in chasing down his enemy,

They reached Succoth, asking for food while in chase of the Midian kings.

Succoth replied, "Catch them first. Until then you will receive not one thing."

Gideon said, "After God gives me victory, this you will regret.

I will return with thorns and briers and tear off your flesh."

He got the same answer in Penuel for the help he did seek.

Gideon said, "After victory, I will tear down your tower piece by piece."

Only fifteen thousand warriors remained of the armies of the allied.

Gideon circled around the caravan east route, taking them by surprise.

After battle, Gideon captured a young man from the Succoth town.

"All seventy-seven officials and elders, write their names down.

Returning to Succoth, you taunted about feeding my exhausted army.

I have returned with thorns and briers. Now you must deal with me."

Gideon also returned to Penuel and killed all the men in town.

Gideon did as he promised and tore the Penuel tower down.

Gideon asked the two kings, the men killed at Tabor, what were they like.

They replied, "They had the look of a king's son standing in plain sight."

Gideon replied, "They were the sons of my mother you put to the sword.

I wouldn't kill you if you didn't kill them as surely lives the Lord."

Gideon turned to his oldest son, Jether, and said, "Lay them to waste."

But Jether didn't draw his sword; he was only a boy and afraid.

"Be a man, kill us yourself, and don't let a boy put us to death."

Killing them both, Gideon took the royal ornaments from their camel's neck.

Then the Israelites wanted Gideon and his heirs to rule.

Gideon replied, "We will not; this is for the Lord God to do.

However, here is what you can do for me.

Give me an earring from the plunder of your enemy."

Gladly they replied, making a joyous sound.

They spread out a cloak, and the plunder weighed forty-three pounds.

Gideon made a sacred ephod like the ones worn by priests.

People began to idolize it, and it became a trap to his family.

With forty years of peace in the lands,

Gideon had much time on his hands.

Gideon had seventy sons born to him with many wives.

He was buried in the grave of his father, Joash, when he died.

After his death, Israel prostituted itself by worshipping images of Baal,

Showing no loyalty to the family of Gideon, also known as Jerubbaal.

(Judg. 7:8–15, Judg. 7:16–25, Judg. 8:1–9, Judg. 8:10–21, Judg. 8:22–27, Judg. 8:29–33)

Vengeance belongs to the Almighty. All the nations being cruel to His people, eventually

God took care of them His way. Gideon asked for food and drink but was denied. What happened to them? What is the reason for being cruel? Because you can? Does it make you feel superior? Are you cruel? Or do you have a giving heart? God knows the answer. The great news is that you can go to God and seek His help, seek His counsel for whatever is troubling you. He is there for all of us if we seek Him earnestly and honestly. Get a Bible you can understand, read four pages per day, and enjoy!

Millstone Judge

Gideon's son, Abimelech, went to Shechem to visit uncles and kin.
He said to them to ask this of the leading citizens,
"Do you want to be ruled by all seventy sons strong?
Or do you want to be ruled by one of your own?
I am blood of your blood and flesh of your flesh.
Of all the seventy sons, I am your very best bet."
So Abimelech's uncles spoke to the citizens and gave his message.
They listened to the proposal and voted in favor of their relative.
They gave him seventy silver coins from Baalberith's temple,
Hiring some reckless troublemakers that agreed to follow him.
In his quest for power, he killed all sixty-nine brothers on one stone.
The youngest of the sixty-nine, Jotham, escaped and hid alone.
Then the leading citizens under the oak called a meeting.
Beside the pillar at Shechem, they decided to make him king.
Jotham climbed Mount Gerizim and shouted a parable verse
About the trees, about the thorn bush, and he shouted a curse.
"May you find joy, Abimelech, and may he find joy in you,
But if not acted in good faith, careful of what Abimelech will do.
May fire come out of you and may it devour each other."
Jotham escaped to Beer because he was afraid of his brother.
After Abimelech ruled three years over Israel in wickedness,
God sent a spirit, stirring up trouble for their punishment.
The citizens of Shechem revolted, setting up an ambush on the hilltop,
Robbing everyone that passed, but someone warned the king of their plot.
Gaal, son of Ebed, and his brothers moved to Shechem one day,
Gaining the confidence in the leading citizens and heads of state.
One day in Shechem at the annual harvest festival party,
Everyone began cursing Abimelech because the wine flowed freely.
Gaal said, "If I were in charge, I would get rid of Abimelech. I would say,
'Go, get some soldiers and come out and fight this very day.'
He is not a true son of Shechem. Who is he?
Why should we listen to him and Zebul his deputy?
Why should we serve him? He is not one of us."
When Zebul heard what Gaal was saying, he was furious.

Zebul told the king, "Gaal and his brothers have a riot intent.
You need to come with your army and make him silent.
Hide in the fields and bring your army at night.
In the morning, attack the city at first light."
Gaal led the leading citizens into battle against his foe.
Many of Shechems's men were wounded and fell by the road.
The next day, the people of Shechem, in the fields a battle raged.
Abimelech warriors cut them down, and they stormed the city gates.
He killed the people, leveled the city, and spread salt was their demise.
Citizens of the tower heard this; in the house of Berith they tried to hide.
Abimelech took an ax, chopped branches, and said, "Do exactly as me.
Pile the branches against the walls of the temple so they can't get free."
Then Abimelech attacked the town of Thebez and captured it.
Having a strong tower inside, the entire population ran inside it.
They barricaded themselves inside and climbed up to the roof.
Abimelech followed to attack and said, "I know what I will do."
As he prepared to set fire to the entrance to maintain his throne,
A woman on the roof crushed his skull, dropping a millstone.
He quickly told his armor bearer, "Take a sword and strike me dead.
'A woman killed Abimelech by a millstone' can never be said."
The armor bearer ran him through with the sword, and Abimelech died.
His army saw his death, disbanded, and went home back to their lives.
God punished Abimelech and the men of Shechem's evil deeds.
Jotham's curse came true, and the parable of the thorn bush and trees.

Did we read this correctly? God sent a spirit to stir trouble? Was it a demon? It won't be the last time God does this. Just wait until we get to 1 Samuel 16:14. Please read Jotham's parable in Judges 9:7–15 for full understanding of his curse. We may think evil tends to get away with so much, but it doesn't. How about recognizing our own sins first and then having faith and patience in God to do His punishing. His justice. Do we point the finger outward instead of inward? Which of us is sinless? Who is casting the first stone? Should we get our house in order before we go rummaging through someone else's home? Pray for strength, patience, guidance, and wisdom to the Lord God for our shortcomings. He will give you more than you can imagine. Guaranteed!

(Judg. 9:1–5, Judg. 9:16–21, Judg. 9:22–30, Judg. 9:34–39, Judg. 9:42–46, Judg. 9:50–56)

Hasty Vow

Again the Israelites did evil in the Lord's sight.

He handed them over to the Philistines and Ammonites.

If the Ammonites sound familiar, you would be correct.

Lot's daughter got her father drunk, and it is he with whom she slept.

But for eighteen years the Israelites were oppressed.

Once again they cried to the Lord to give them rest.

"We have sinned; we have served another god before you."

God replied, "When you cry out, do I not come to your rescue?

You have served other gods when you were not put to the test.

Now go and cry out to the gods you serve in your hour of distress."

Israel said, "Punish us as you see fit." It was their plea.

"We have sinned but rescue us today from our enemy."

The Lord God was grieved by their pain and misery.

"They have put aside their foreign god; now they serve me."

The armies of Ammon gathered for war camped in Gilead.

The leaders of Gilead said, "Whoever begins the fight will be head."

Jephthah was chased out, but it was nothing he had done.

Jephthah, a great warrior, was run out by Gilead's other sons.

Jephthah's half brothers said, "Our father's inheritance will not go to you.

You are not one of us. Your mother is a prostitute."

A band of worthless rebels soon followed Jephthah in Tob's lands.

The elders of Gilead sent word to him, for the army to command.

Jephthah said, "You ran me out,

Kept me from my father's house.

Now in trouble, you come asking me to lead you.

And if I lead in battle, you tell me I can rule."

He sent messengers to the king of Ammon. "Why do you come to fight?"

The king of Ammon answered, "My land was stolen by the Israelites.

None of it belongs to you. Now give it back peaceably."

Jephthah replied, "Soon hard troubles came after crossing the Red Sea.

After fighting many kings and years of misery and grief,

The Lord our God gave us these lands because of our belief.

Israel has been here for three hundred years. Now you want it back?

We have not sinned against you, but you wrong me with an attack.

Whatever your god Chemosh gives you, you can keep in your hands.

Let the Lord, who is judge, decide for right of Gilead's lands"

The spirit of God came upon Jephthah, and he made a vow in haste.

Later this vow from his mouth will leave a painful and bitter taste.

"When I return in triumph over the Ammonites, if I am granted victory,

I will sacrifice a burnt offering, whatever comes out of my house to meet me."

Jephthah crushed the Ammonites; about twenty towns were destroyed.

Returning home, his daughter came out to meet him dancing in joy.

He cried out because he knew what this means,

A vow to God, a sacrifice as a burnt offering.

"No, father, the Lord gave you victory. Please do not grieve.

Let me go to the hills for two months, and your vow you will keep."

His daughter wept in the hills for two months with her friends.

Her father kept his vow he made, and she died a virgin.

Jephthah judged for six years, and he was buried in a Gilead town.

Three more judges led before it was time for Samson to lead, Sampson the strong.

Does the story sound familiar? How about Joseph's brothers Genesis 37? Or even the last story in Judges 9 of Abimelech? How many times has God saved the Israelites? Each time faith is lost, they backslide. How many times have you cried out to the Father to save you? How many times have we put Him on the back burner for other items? How many promises have we made without thinking of the consequences? "God, if you do this this, then I will do this." Spiritual deals never work. Make promises to yourself; if not, God will hold you to your word. Our tongue can be very dangerous. A very old saying: think before you speak.

(Gen. 19:30–38 (origin of the Ammonites), Judg. 10:6–17, Judg. 11:1–3, Judg. 11:4–8, Judg. 11:12–14, Judg. 11:15–22, Judg. 11:26–27, Judg. 11:24, Judg. 11:29–31, Judg. 11:32–35, Judg. 11:36–40, Judg. 12:8–13)

Biblical Superman

The Philistines for forty years oppressed the Israelites' life.

Again they did evil in the Lord's sight.

Samson father's name was Manoah,

From the tribe of Dan living in Zorah.

His wife was unable to become pregnant; her womb was bare.

An angel appeared and said, "You will have a son, so take care.

He will be dedicated to God from birth as a Nazirite.

This means you should be careful and live a clean life.

Do not drink wine, alcohol, or eat any forbidden food.

You will give birth to a son, and cutting his hair is disapproved."

Not knowing at the time

His hair is strength divine.

The angel of the Lord appeared to her twice,

Each time telling her to make sure she eats and drinks right.

The second time, Manoah said, "I will prepare a goat for you to eat."

The angel replied, "I will not eat, nor my name will I speak."

From the rock's altar, flames shot up toward the skies

Right before Manoah and his wife's eyes.

Manoah said to his wife, "We shall surely die."

"He told us wonderful news and miracles," she replied.

His wife said, "He told us about our son's life,

About him being dedicated to God as a Nazirite,

The famous of all judges, the biblical Superman,

The story of Samson, the last judge in the land."

As Samson grew up, he was blessed.

God was preparing him for his life's test.

One day he saw a woman and told his parents, "Get her for me.

I was in Timnath. A Philistine woman caught my eye, and I want to marry."

His parents objected to having a pagan Philistine as a wife.

"Isn't there even one woman in our tribe among all the Israelites?"

Samson stood steadfast. "Get her. She is the one for me."

His parents didn't know it was God creating an opportunity.

As Samson and his parents journeyed toward Timnath lands,

A young lion attacked Samson, and he ripped it apart with his hands.

He didn't tell his father or mother what he had done.

The spirit came strong upon him, God's Nazirite son.

Samson talked to the woman, and he was very satisfied.

He was pleased knowing she would become his wife.

Later, returning to Timnath, he turned to look at the lion's body,

And in it he found a swarm of bees that had made some honey.

He scooped some honey and ate it along the way,

Gave some to his parents, but from where he did not say.

Samson had a party, which was custom for a young man,

And his father was busy making final wedding plans.

They chose thirty men to be by Samson's side.

Samson said, "I have a riddle before I marry my bride.

If you can solve my riddle during the seven days of celebration.

I will give thirty robes and thirty sets of clothes as dedication.

If you can't answer, you must give the same to me."

They replied, "Let's hear your riddle," then they agreed.

"Out of the eater came forth some meat.

Out from the strong came something sweet."

Three days later, they could not figure it out,

Still puzzled with what Samson's riddle was all about.

On the fourth day, still with not a clue, they said to Samson's wife,

"Entice him to tell you or we'll burn the house and take your life."

Samson's wife, sobbing, said, "You hate me. You don't love me.

You've given my people a riddle, and you won't tell me."

"I haven't given it to my father or mother," Samson replied.

For the entire seven days of celebration, all she did was cry.

He finally told her the answer on the seventh day.

She told her people. Samson didn't know he was betrayed.

On the seventh day, the thirty men answered correctly.

"What is stronger than a lion and what's sweeter than honey?"

Samson said, "If my heifer was not plowed,

My riddle you would not have solved."

The spirit of the Lord came upon Samson powerfully.

He went to the town of Ashkelon and killed thirty men easily.

Thirty men's belongings and clothes he took because of his bet
And gave it to the thirty men because his riddle they did interpret.
Samson returned home to his parents because of his rage,
But his wife was given to the best man from his wedding day.
This is part I of the biblical Superman.
Part II is tales of strength in the Philistine's land.
Tales of vengeance and wrath.
This is Samson's war path.

Haven't we heard stories about incredible feats of strength? Most times, it was either drug enhanced or emotionally induced to save someone's life. Then again, what can't God do? Remember, He can use anyone. As a man, women are absolutely beautiful, but all that looks good to me may not be good for me. This is just as true for a woman. Acting on impulse instead of asking God first can lead to disappointments. How many of us act on eye candy? We buy or want the first attractive item/person we see before we research. Impulse, we all are guilty of that. Are you seeing a pattern about not trusting God?

(Judg. 13:1–5, Judg. 13:13–18, Judg. 13:23–25, Judg. 14:1–9, Judg. 14:10–19)

The Three Hundred
Tails of Superman

Later on during the harvest of wheat,

Samson went to his wife's room. He wanted to sleep.

He took a young goat as a present to his wife.

He wanted to consummate his marriage that night.

But her father wouldn't let Samson in,

And this is when the Philistines' trouble begins.

He said, "I thought you hate her, so I gave her to your best man.

Her younger sister is beautiful; you can still be a lucky man."

In rage because now his marriage wasn't true,

Samson said, "This time don't blame me for what I do."

Three hundred foxes he caught; in his mind, his vengeance was sound.

Tails tied in pairs with torches and burned their grain to the ground.

He let the foxes run through field to ease his pain,

Burning all, including the sheaves and uncut grain.

The Philistines demanded, "Who did this to our lands?"

"Samson," they replied. "His wife was given to the best man."

The Philistines took his wife and her father and burned them alive.

Samson vowed, "I won't rest until I take many Philistines' lives."

With all his strength, his wife and father-in-law he couldn't save.

Attacking Philistines with great fury, then he went and lived in a cave.

The Philistines camped in Judah, and the people asked, "Why attack us?"

The Philistines said, "We will capture Samson and do what he did to us."

Three thousand men went to Samson and said, "They rule over us. Can't you see?"

Samson replied, "I only did to them what they did to me."

"We have come to tie you up and hand you over peaceably."

Samson said, "All right but promise that you won't kill me."

They tied him with two ropes, and at Lehi when they arrived,

The Philistines were shouting, "We have received their prize."

Samson snapped the ropes, picked up a jawbone, time to kill.

He laid to waste one thousand Philistines and boasted on Jawbone Hill.

"With a jawbone of a donkey,
I have piled them in heaps."
Crying out to the Lord, "Now must I die of thirst for all you achieved?
Will I fall into the hands of the Philistines, those who don't believe?"
So God caused water to gush out from a hollow place.
Samson was revived, and it is still in Lehi to this day.
Later in Gaza, with a prostitute Samson spent the night.
The men of Gaza gathered; come morning there would be a fight.
Keeping quiet at the town gates, they waited all night,
But Samson stayed in bed only until midnight.
He arose, picked up the town gates, not worried about their plot,
Carried them on his shoulders with the bar and post up to the hilltop.
This would not be the end of Samson's fight,
Next he will meet Superman's kryptonite.

I wonder what happened to the foxes. Rage, vengeance, and anger can lead to a path of destruction. How about these two scriptures, Rom. 12:19 and Prov. 26:27? "Before you embark on a journey of revenge, dig two graves." Do you seek revenge on others that have done you wrong? Do you have all the facts? And the bigger of the questions, is it worth it? Think about the time, effort, and energy spent on meaningless revenge. Sounds exhausting! All will be revealed in the next poem, "Superman's Kryptonite."

(Judg. 15:1–5, Judg. 15:6–9, Judg. 15:9–20, Judg. 16:1–3)

Superman's Kryptonite

Later, Samson fell in love with a woman. Delilah was her name.

After experiencing her power, Samson will never be the same.

The rulers of Philistine went to her and said, "Entice him to tell you.

Find out how he can be overpowered and tied, and we will reward you.

These are the answers we seek,

We will pay 1,100 pieces of silver each."

Delilah asked, "What makes you strong and how to tie you securely?"

Samson said, "Seven new un-dried bowstrings, and I will become weak."

Delilah did as Samson said, with men hidden waiting to spring the trap.

She cried out, "The Philistines are here!" and all the bowstrings Samson snapped.

She tried again and again,

Trying to solve the riddle of Superman.

She tried with seven new ropes that had never been used.

Again Samson made her look like a fool.

She tried with fabric being woven in his hair with seven braids.

And again, this was easy, and Samson escaped.

Now came the enticing part.

She played with his heart.

"How can you say that you love me

When three times you made fun of me?"

She tormented him with her nagging until he was sick of it.

He finally broke down and said, "I will tell you my secret.

If my hair was cut, the source of my strength would leave."

After waiting so long, Delilah knew his words she could believe.

Delilah sent for the Philistine rulers to come back one more time.

"Samson has told me his secret, and tonight he is all mine."

With Samson asleep in her lap, she called to cut off the seven braids.

His head shaved, his strength gone, Samson couldn't escape.

When he awoke, he had to face his own demise.

The Philistines captured him and gouged out his eyes.

They took Samson to Gaza where he had uprooted the city gate.

The Lord did not completely leave Samson to his dying fate.

Samson was bound with bronze chains,

In prison now, forced to grind grains.

"Our God has delivered our enemy into our hands.

The one that slew our people and laid waste to the lands."

These were the words the Philistines said about Samson's downfall.

Samson thought he would never again hear the Lord's call.

Drunk now, the people shouted, "Bring Samson out for our amusement!"

Leading him by the hand, Samson was brought out by a young servant.

Samson said, "Place my hands on the pillars so I can rest."

Then he prayed to God, "Just once more let me be blessed."

With three thousand people being entertained,

He prayed, for the last of his strength remained.

"Let me pay them back for the loss of my eyes.

Give me the strength, and with them I will die."

Pushing the pillars while praying, the temple fell at one time.

Samson killed more when he died than in all of his lifetime.

Samson judged Israel for twenty years with passion and fire,

Brought down by kryptonite's charm, named Delilah.

Is a woman's touch more than the blessings of God? Or a man's? Eye candy again in Judg. 14:1. Should we not try to find out a person's character and faith in God first? Are these features just as desirable as the physical? Most of the time spent with your spouse is not spent having sex. Find out what lies beneath the pleasant features and a soothing touch. Have you fell to your desires? A nice touch? A pretty face? Most people have much to offer under the surface. It is beneficial to find out what they are before you succumb to your desires. It could be your kryptonite. Just ask Samson. Would you tell God's secret to your strength?

(Judg. 16:4–5, Judg. 16:6–14, Judg. 16:17–21, Judg. 16:21–25, Judg. 16:26–30)

Pieces of Twelve

A Levi man brought home a woman from Bethlehemjudah to be his concubine.

Eventually she did wrong and was unfaithful during this time.

She left and went back home to her father's place.

After four months, he went to her to plead his case.

He took with him two saddled donkeys and his servant.

Her father said, "Stay awhile. It will be good time spent."

For three days he enjoyed her father's hospitality.

On the fourth, he was ready to return to the hill country.

But her father said, "Please eat before you leave."

They sat, ate, and her father said, "Stay another night please."

On day five, her father said, "Please eat and leave this afternoon."

They sat, ate, and her father said, "It's late. It will be dark soon.

Tomorrow you can get up early and be on your way."

The man was determined not to be persuaded the same way.

He would not be sidetracked, the man had no doubt.

He saddled his two donkeys with his concubine and headed out.

His servant said, "Let's stop at this Jebusite town for the night.

"No," his master said, "in this foreign town, there are no Israelites."

So they went on.

Soon the setting of the sun.

They came to Gibeah, a town in the land of Benjamin.

Stopping to rest, thinking someone will take them in,

They rested in the town's square.

Not a soul seemed to care.

Later, an old man retuning from work who was from the same hill country

Saw the travelers resting in the square, said, "You can come home with me.

You are welcome at my house; I have all that you need.

Whatever you do, don't stay the night in the square please."

While enjoying themselves, wicked men surrounded the house.

They pounded the door, yelling to bring the stranger out.

They were yelling to bring him out so they can have sex.

The old man stepped out and said, "Please don't disrespect.

I will bring out my virgin daughter and his concubine.

Do with them as you please. That will be fine."

But they didn't listen.

They were on a mission.

He pushed his concubine out the door without a fight.

They had sex and abused her throughout the night.

She found her way back to the house; they finally let her go.

His concubine fell in the doorway with her hand on the threshold.

He said, "Get up, let's go, it's time to go home."

There wasn't a sound, not a word or even a moan.

When he returned home to the hill countries,

He took a knife and cut his concubine in twelve pieces.

And it was so that all twelve tribes saw this horrible act.

"Not since we left Egypt have we seen such an attack."

Soon the Israelites will know the tribe of Benjamin did this.

Now they must unite against one of their own to be punished.

Sound familiar with "send them out for sex"? Gen. 19:5–8 is the story of Lot in Sodom. Not all places you stop are friendly, and sometimes you need to push on to your destination. How many times have you ended up in the wrong spot and things went wrong? Or you were delayed too long. Maybe not to this extreme, but it was an unpleasant experience. Will you be persuaded or delayed from reading the Word? Will you be persuaded or delayed from Jesus? My theme again: four pages per day and a Bible you can understand. Keep reading!

(Judg. 19:1–4, Judg. 19:5–11, Judg. 19:12–21, Judg. 19:22–26, Judg. 19:26–30)

Concubine's War

As one man, the children of Israel united as one

To battle against their brother, one of the twelve sons.

At Mizpeh, they gathered together the entire community,

With the exception of the tribe of Benjamin, now their enemy.

Then the Israelites said, "Tell us of this horrible crime."

The man said, "They raped and killed my concubine

In the house were we stayed, rested, and were fed.

They planned to kill me and raped her until she was dead.

Then I cut her into twelve pieces and sent them to all of you.

Now tell me, children of Israel, what will you do?"

Rising as one, they said, "None will leave. Lots will be cast.

The men responsible will pay, down to the very last."

Messengers sent asking, "What was done among your people?"

"A terrible thing. Give us the men. We shall purge this evil."

But the tribe of Benjamin didn't listen to the Israelites,

Instead, they gathered together preparing for a fight.

Before battle, Israel went to Bethel to the Lord with a question to ask.

"Which tribe should go first? Which of the tribes shall attack?"

God said, "Judah should go first because you have prayed."

But Benjamin's warriors killed twenty-two thousand on the battlefield that day.

Asking God on day two, "Do we fight our brothers in this mess?"

God said, "Go up against them." In other words, yes.

On the second day, eighteen thousand Israelites fell to the sword.

Again, up to Bethel, weeping in the presence of the Lord.

They fasted that day until evening,

Presenting to the Lord with offerings.

The Lord said, "Go, for tomorrow I will deliver them to you."

With ambush in place, on day three, the Benjamites were through.

A well-constructed attack that worked with precision.

The Benjamites were defeated, and the end of the division.

On that day, eighteen thousand of Benjamin's strongest warriors died in battle.

The six hundred remaining retreated to the Rock of Rimmon. They were rattled.

The Israelites returned and slaughtered everything in all the town,

The people, the livestock, and everything they found.

And to make sure this evil wasn't unbound,

They burned all the towns to the ground.

Going back to Bethel, crying to the Lord, "What have we done?

We are missing a tribe. The few that remain have no sons."

They called a meeting at Mizpeh to put this to rest

But vowed whoever didn't attend would be put to death.

"Which of us didn't attend the assembly?"

It was found it was Jabesh-gilead.

"Kill everyone in the town who is not a virgin.

This way the six hundred Benjamites can begin again"

A peace delegation told the six hundred to go home, "Because you now have wives."

But it was only four hundred virgins, which left a gap for the two hundred others that survived.

"The remaining two hundred, go to the vineyards and hide,

And there you will find a bride.

The festival that goes from Bethel to Shechem,

In Shiloh along the east road, there take your men.

When the women come out to dance that day,

Jump out from hiding, and one of them you can take.

When the fathers and brothers come to us in protest,

We will say to them, 'Please be sympathetic.'

You are not guilty because you did not actually give them away."

The Benjamites did as they were told and took one as they celebrated.

The people departed tribe by tribe and family by family.

Again twelve tribes and again a complete community.

Extreme measures to send out a message, don't you think? But wasn't this part of God's plan, to purge evil from the land in the book of Deuteronomy? Aren't we all stronger united as one? Even though the eleven tribes fought against their brother Benjamin, the power of forgiveness is amazing. It is wonderful how God touches us even when we are in the heat of battle. Two emotions that nearly destroyed the tribes were rage and pride. Do you allow rage to rule you, injuring another? Does your pride prevent you from apologizing? Can you truly forgive and move on with love? We have not made it to the New Testament, but Matt. 18:21–22 should be the standard to forgiving. We can only do this by allowing Jesus into our hearts and souls.

We are moving on from the book of Judges, but that doesn't mean not to read the entire book. A story about idolatry in chapters 17 and 18 reveals much about the tribe of Benjamin. Of course I have to encourage you to read four pages per day and to have a Bible translation you can understand. Keep reading God's Word, keep praying, keep the faith, and learn to forgive.

Next we move on the last book of the Bible in this series of biblical poetry. Thus far, I hope you truly have enjoyed reading my work of the first eight books of His Word. I sincerely hope your journey to Christ is rewarding and that He continues to bless you for your faithfulness. God wants us to prosper, He wants us to be happy, and like a father, He wants the best for us. Now, He never said it would be easy or we wouldn't be tested, but He is the answer.

The next series of poems is a prelude to the book of Ruth. These are about love, friendship, loyalty, respect, and genuine love. The first two are poems I wrote for my mother expressing my love for her. One is for all mothers for Mothers' Day. My mom has been a true inspiration in my life's journey to Christ. We all should be influential to others' spiritual growth. Here are some questions to ponder. Don't you at least want your friend to make it to heaven? Your son, daughter, spouse, and the people you love? Do you think God will hold us accountable for not helping others with their journey to Him?

Poems

Son's Pride

What can we say about our mom?
This may sound funny coming from her sons,
With all the things she had to endure.
We watched her grow and watched her mature.
We watched her grow and obtain knowledge.
We watched her educate and graduate from college.
We watched her struggle to make ends meet,
Beating the odds keeping two sons off the streets,
She did this by the fair and firm hand.
She did this by following God's plan.
We are honored with the lady that gave us life,
Even when we had to do our homework twice,
Or the times we couldn't hang with the boys on the block.
Now we know it kept us from being chased by the cops.
Or the times she pushed us to stay in school
And dressed us nice not to look like a fool.
Now from boys to men is who she raised.
She made sure she gave God all the praise.
We can go on and on about everything our mom can do,
But all we can say, "Mom, your sons are proud of you."
Dedicated to mom from me and my older brother.

Mom the Matriarch

To all mothers.

Who was it that gave birth to thee?

Who is the matriarch of the family tree?

All the family secrets she keeps,

Hangs on to them until God calls her to sleep.

Who was there when you called out in pain?

Who wiped the tears and said, "There's no shame

For trying your best even if you didn't win"?

Dusted you off and said, "Hold up your chin."

Whose name did you call when feeling blue?

And she just held you until you felt new,

Just rocked you in her arms until the tears were gone,

Held you tightly and softly sang a song.

Who was it that told you to stay in school?

And who did they call when you acted a fool?

Who stayed on you to graduate?

And whose name did you call because you appreciate

All the nights your homework was checked,

Then told to redo it because it wasn't correct?

Now here you stand with degree in hand,

Grown to be a fine young man.

Who gave you all the recipes to cook?

Secret ingredients not found in a book.

Who told you to pull up your pants and comb your hair?

During adolescence when you seemed not to care,

Who told you how to keep your clothes tight

And that there's only trouble late at night?

Now about your newborn, who do you seek for advice

That has your problem solved before the end of the night"

Now raising kids of your own,

You use the same remedies in your home

That you were shown when you were young,

Taking nasty medicines, trying to make it fun,

Shown to you by the matriarch.

At first you resisted; now you take part.

Stories told to your kids while you eavesdrop,

About how you burnt your fingers on the hot pot,

Or about your first haircut at the local shop,

Or your first touchdown because you couldn't be stopped.

How about the time you had your first date?

And how your socks didn't match because you were late?

You listened to every word that was spoke,

And now a lump forms in your throat.

It is said they can't raise a boy to a man,

But who better to show you how to treat a woman?

Who better than the foundation of man?

She's the only one who understands her man,

Knows him better than he,

Understands the wants and needs.

You bow your head and only one name to think of,

Just Mom giving you all her love.

Open Heart

My definition of a good man in this poem.

It doesn't make me right or it doesn't make me wrong.

To me a man is someone that handles his biz,

Raises his own and sometimes someone else's kids,

Always takes care of everyone before himself,

Not too proud to bend his knees and ask God for help,

Always praises God for the blessings in his life,

Thankful for his family, his kids, and his wife,

Always a working man and tries not to miss a day,

Except for playing hooky with his wife for a play date.

Educates his kids on making an honest living

And sometimes the experience is worth more than winning.

Explains the importance of communication and unity,

The strength in support and the foundation of family,

The protector, provider, the fair and firm hand,

The educator, the rock and the example of a good man.

Shows his son all the sports to play,

And his daughter, a man will treat her the right way.

So if you are a man,

This poem you will understand.

A man does this and many more great things.

If this is you, open your heart and let it sing.

I am a good man

Living in God's plan.

Days of the Week

The question was asked,

"What's the occasion?

You gave me flowers.

It's not my birthday.

It's not a holiday.

Then what?"

I said.

"It's Thursday.

Let me explain,

Sunday, the first day of the week,

Means I give my love to you first.

Monday, the second day of the week,

Means my love to you is second to none.

Tuesday, the third day of the week,

Means I love you three time more.

Wednesday, hump day,

Means your love gets me over the hump.

Thursday, ladies' night,

Means you are the only lady in my life.

Friday, happy hour,

Means that every hour that passes, I am happy with our love.

Saturday, the day of rest,

Means my love does not rest for you.

And I can't wait for Sunday to start loving you all over again.

Any more questions?"

Blessed

Define a friend for me.
Someone who is there with me.
When in trouble, your friend is there,
Maybe in trouble with you
Or preventing you from getting into trouble.
When family is ill,
Your friend is there.
When you celebrate,
Your friend is there.
When you cry,
Your friend is there.
The birth of your child,
Your friend is there.
Your marriage,
Your divorce,
Your housewarming,
All your life,
At your funeral,
A true friend is
Present.

High-Low

When they go low, we go high.

Even when they try to make me fight,

I smile to hide the pain inside.

They don't acknowledge me out of despite.

I keep my chin up and hold my head high.

I know their conscience says it's not right,

Trying to bring me down to their size.

When they go low, we get blessings from the Most High.

I brush my shoulders off with ease.

Then I shake the dust off my feet.

Sometimes I bite down and grit my teeth,

But they can't bring me to my knees.

Only to God just to hear me speak,

Praying He keeps me strong with what I need.

When they go low, we keep praying to the Most High.

They continually insult my intelligence,

But they only show their ignorance,

And they keep coming because of arrogance.

I stand tall, unshaken with confidence,

Enduring all with God's patience.

Don't they know God gives me guidance?

When they go low, we get wisdom from the Most High.

They don't know how much I can take.

Then they place more on my plate.

But God is still with me, for heaven's sake,

Because every day in prayer I partake.

They can't bring me down in disgrace

Because I live by His mercy and His grace.

When they go low, we call on the Most High.

Here I Stand

What will I say when I stand before the King?

Will I say I am yours, I am the offering?

Will I kneel and bow in silence,

Asking for forgiveness as I repent?

Can I stand as His eyes pierce through my soul?

Thinking on my sins from young to old,

Will those sins cause me to cringe and fold?

Do they have a grip on me and not let go?

A feeling of shame as all comes to the light,

Will the angels be disgusted and take flight?

Will all my sins cause others to look away?

Will those who know me look at me in a different way?

When I stand before the King,

Can I give praises and use my voice to sing?

Can I join others in a thunderous song?

Will we sing together, "We have made it home"?

But I am working to become a better man,

And want to say this when I stand:

"Here I stand.

I stand to be a better Christian.

I stand to be a fisher of men.

I stand to love my neighbor.

I stand to be in God's favor.

I will be a witness to His power.

I will spread His Gospel hour by hour.

I will shout until I reach the mountaintop.

I will praise Him until the mighty seas stop.

Here I stand.

I stand to love my enemies.

I stand for the weak and meek.

I stand for those who can't stand.

I stand to be a better man.

I stand for those who are afraid.

I stand for those who lost their way.

I stand for a brighter day.

Here I stand.

I stand tall in praying.

I stand tall in fasting.

I stand tall in witnessing.

I stand tall in worshipping.

I stand tallest on bended knee.

Father, here I stand for your mercy.

Jesus died on the cross for me.

God sacrificed His Son for me.

He died for my sins.

Jesus died for us to see Him again.

Here I stand in Jesus's name.

Amen.

What will you say when you stand before the King of Kings? I truly want to say something like this, or perhaps my journey will bring further glory to His name. We all want to make the Father proud of us. But are we doing all we can in the world that values self-pride more than anything? The phrase "I got mines" is the norm, but what about helping others? When we fall, who will be there to pick us up? Will you help others when they fall? Or will you say, "It's not my concern; it doesn't affect me"? As Christians, we live in this world, but shouldn't let the world influence us away from God's teachings.

Think about this. If a loved one was in trouble, wouldn't you want someone to come to their aid? How would you feel if someone could help, but they only stood around taking pictures with their cell phones? Are you that person? When does it affect you? Should we not be the example people should follow? Remember, Jesus died for us all. He stood for us. He helped us. The Bible teaches us times will become worse before the Lord of Hosts returns. How bad is it now? Please understand, my journey with you needs just as much improvement as the next person's. Learn to pray for each other and with each other. Pray for your neighbors and for the people you think are against you. Reach out to them to show them that there is a better way. A better path. The path is Jesus. We all stumble, fall, and sometimes get off the path, but that is why we need each other. To pick each other up, to put each other back on the path. What will you say when you stand?

Ruth

This book in the Bible is only four chapters but covers so many different themes, such as love, faith, loyalty, integrity, friendship, family, kindness, and God's blessings. There are many others to name, but Ruth demonstrates God's impartiality of faithfulness. How about this one, great-grandmother of David, an ancestor to Jesus. And the man she married, his ancestor was a former prostitute from Jericho. Remember the poem "Twelve Stones and a Prostitute"? Yes, you guessed correctly, it was Rahab. Do you think Rahab knew she would be kin to Christ? Or Ruth? Now, which one of you still believes God *does not* use who is faithful or who He wants? What a God we serve!

Ruth starts in tragedy but ends in triumph. A great example of family values, friendship, and faithfulness. We all need to read the underlying themes more than once for great understanding. This is a testament of true family and friendship. We may not see the finish line or what impact we have in our bloodline, but God does. He has a plan for us all if we listen and follow Him. Ruth says that she has nothing and finished with having a grandchild. The community speaks to her and says, "Your daughter-in-law who loves you and has been better to you than seven sons." What a statement!

Call Me Mara

Elimelech, husband of Naomi, died.

Their two sons carried on with their lives.

Their two sons, Mahlon and Chilion were their names.

The wives they married, Orpah and Ruth were their names.

Both Mahlon and Chilion died about ten years later.

Returning to Judah because the Lord gave the land favor.

Journeying home, Naomi said, "Go back to your mother's home.

May the Lord bless and reward you, but He's left me all alone."

She blessed them, kissed them, said good-bye, and they started to weep.

They replied, "No, it is you we want to go with, and it is you we want to keep."

"I can't provide you husbands to continue the family name.

I am too old to marry again. Leave me to my shame.

And if I could have sons, they could refuse you to marry.

Things are bitter because the Lord raised his fist against me."

Orpah kissed Naomi good-bye, and they started to weep.

Ruth refused to leave; she clung to Naomi very tightly.

"Look," Naomi said, "your sister-in-law left. This is your task."

But Ruth replied, "No, please don't ask me to leave and turn back.

Wherever you go, I will go. This is my path.

Wherever you live, I live, for as long as it lasts.

Your people will be my people, and your God will be mine.

Wherever you die, I will die, until we are buried in our lifetime.

May God punish me if anything but death will divide us apart."

Ruth serious, Naomi silent, and then they began to depart.

They continued on their journey, not knowing their fate,

Receiving a warm welcome when they reached Bethlehem's gate.

"Is it really Naomi?" the women asked because they were pleased.

"Yes, but call me Mara. The Almighty has brought misfortune on me.

I went away full and happy.

Now I return with arms empty.

The Almighty has sent such a tragedy upon me.

I've suffered. Why the name Naomi should you call me."

Accompanied by Ruth, they returned at the start of the barley harvest. Eventually both of them will realize that the Lord God will soon bless.

This is a very short chapter. Please read all of chapter 1. Amazingly, some say the book could have been called Naomi. Do these words come to mind: faithful, friendship, loyalty, and pain? This, for me, shows how strong women can be; in the midst of losing all, they endured. Woman or man, would this have broken you? Would you curse God? It was a true test of faith and will to go on. Would you stick by your in-law? Can you name a family member or friend you are that close to? If we have one person such as this in our lifetime, we are blessed. Hold on to them and never let go. Of course Jesus will never leave, but I'm speaking of an earthly friend.

Grains of Redemption

Ruth said, "Let me go into the field to pick stalks left behind.

I will do this for anyone who wishes to treat me kind."

As it happens, she found herself in the field of her relative and kin.

This is where Ruth's interesting story of redemption begins.

Greeting the harvesters, Boaz said, "The Lord be with you,"

And the harvesters replied, "May the Lord bless you."

"Who does that young woman belong to?" Boaz asked the overseer.

"She came this morning and wanted to gather behind the harvesters.

She came back with Naomi and has been hard at work all day."

Boaz went over to Ruth; he had a few words to say.

"I warned the young men not to treat you roughly,

And drink from my well whenever you are thirsty."

She fell at his feet, thanked him, and asked, "Why do I deserve this kindness?"

Boaz replied, "I know what you've done for Naomi, showing unselfishness.

You live with strangers and have left all that you have.

May the Lord God above bless you going down this path."

"Your words bring comfort. I am not your worker," she replied.

"May I continue to please you and find favor in your eyes."

"Come over here and dip your bread in some of this wine,"

Boaz invited her to eat with the harvesters during mealtime.

Boaz ordered his men to leave her be and purposely drop sheaves.

"She can gather all she wants and have enough when she leaves."

Ruth went back to town with the barley she gathered all day.

Naomi said, "Where did you gather all this for goodness sake?"

Ruth said, "I worked in the fields of Boaz, as I remember."

Naomi said, "He is our close relative, a family redeemer."

Then Ruth said, "Boaz told me to come back until the harvest is complete."

"Good," Naomi said. "Do as he says where you'll be safe and free."

Ruth stayed for the barley and wheat harvest.

As this story continues, God will reward and bless.

As you continue to read, who says hard work doesn't pay off? Does this sort of kindness exist today? The term today is called "pay it forward." We do hear about it but not too much. Sometimes your reputation can precede you in a positive light. What kind of work/personal reputation do you have? Do you allow rumors to affect how you treat others? There are times we may think to ourselves, *I heard about them*, and already have a negative perception of someone. Or "I heard this or that" and think a person has everything together, only to find out the opposite. Should we not, as Christians, observe for ourselves and ask God to give us wisdom to make a decision? Again, patience, guidance, and wisdom are very important in our spiritual growth.

Famous Bloodline

"Boaz has been very kind by letting you gather grain.

Now, do as I tell you, and your life will never be the same.

Tonight, he will be twinning barley on the threshing floor.

Bathe, put on perfume, don your best clothes before you leave this door.

Don't let Boaz see you until after he finishes eating and drinking.

Then uncover his feet and lie down where he is sleeping."

Ruth did all that Naomi said,

And at his feet is where she made her bed.

In the middle of the night, he awoke and found a woman lying at his feet.

"I am your servant Ruth. Now spread the corner of your covering over me."

"Bless you, for you haven't gone for a younger man, rich or poor.

You are showing more loyalty; I'll give you what you are asking for.

You are a virtuous woman, and all in town will know this.

It's true I am family, but I'm not the closet of your relatives.

In the morning, I will talk to him, but tonight here you will stay.

I will tell him of your situation and find out what he will say."

She laid at his feet all night but left before sunrise.

"No one must know a woman was here to be recognized."

Boaz said, "Don't go back to your mother-in-law with your hands empty.

Bring me your cloak. Spread it out. I'll give you six scoops of barley."

Ruth went back and told Naomi everything Boaz had to say.

Naomi said, "Be patient. Boaz won't rest until it is settled this day."

Boaz went to the city's gate and took a seat.

He saw the redeemer and said, "Come sit next to me."

Boaz said, "Naomi is back from Moab and selling Elimelech's land.

You have first rights, but if you don't buy it, I'll take it off your hands.

Your purchase also requires the Moabite Ruth for you to marry.

She hasn't any sons to carry on the bloodline or name of the family."

At first hearing of the land, the family redeemer agreed.

"After hearing of Ruth, it would endanger my estate to proceed."

He took off a sandal, gave it Boaz as custom for purchase rights.

Boaz said, "I will redeem it, and the Moabite widow will be my wife.

To all the elders, you are witnesses to the purchase of the property.

She can have a son to carry on the name and inherit it to the family."

They replied, "We are witnesses and may the Lord bless you.

May the Lord make Ruth like Rachel and Leah in all that she do."

Boaz took Ruth home because all transactions were done.

Ruth became his wife, and the Lord blessed her with a son.

Women of the town said, "Let the child be famous and restore your youth,

And your daughter-in-law has been better than seven sons because she is true."

Obed was his name, father of Jesse, father of David's bloodline,

And David is the ancestor of Jesus, the most famous of all time.

When this story began, did you think it would end in triumph? Well it did. This bloodline gave birth to our Father Jesus. We do not know who will be in our family tree descendants. All we should do is love them and give them the best we can. Teach them about God and to love others as you love yourself. We should help family members when in need. Sometimes it is difficult and stressful, but it is the right thing to do. Of course, this is understanding that we are not to be taken advantage of. When was the last time you helped a family member? Or a stranger? When was the last time you did a selfless act? This doesn't always involve money; it could be food, clothes, or shelter.

I truly hope my poetry has encouraged you to read God's Word and that it touched poetry lovers. I know I didn't give the whole story in my poetry but more of a summary of the stories. I want you to read His words from start to finish. My poetry is just another avenue to reach a different audience or for those of you seeking to bring them to Christ. You can use this work for the younger audience as stories to raise their interest in God, or for those of you that just enjoy poetry. I have used God's words and worked diligently not to go off course from what He has written. I used as the King James Version but ask you to use a translation you understand and enjoy reading. He has given me the gift of poetry, and I want to give back to anyone, helping them to the Father. I hope I have done that for you.

This book is different from other spiritual/faith poetry books. As stated, take your Bible and the poetry, and you can read for yourself. Also the commentary and questions at the end of most pieces are to spark you to look at your journey toward Christ and your life. I also wanted to touch on some stories that seemed to have been forgotten about or not preached about as much as the familiar ones, which hopefully touches your heart to pick up your Bible and read for yourself. Just enjoy four pages per day reading His Word. That's what it's all about, helping each other to the Father.

The titles of my pieces I truly had fun with, in my attempt to keep you guessing about the poem, such as "Busin Bricks," Biblical Superman," and "Stiff Neck," but once you read the poem and His words, the title make sense. I wish you all happiness with the Father and with each other. May the Lord of all creation give you blessings beyond your imagination and keep you close to His heart. Thank you so much for allowing me to share with you the poetry God has allowed me to write. It is my honor.

Closing

In loving memory of Ervin Smith

Dear kind and wonderful Father,

Please bless anyone who reads this book.

Let them find the love you have shown me.

Keep them safe.

Keep them close to you.

Bless them generously.

Show them the path to your light.

Keep that path lit brightly.

Guide them to your eternal kingdom.

Fill their soul with your spirit.

Give them patience.

Give them wisdom.

Give them love.

Most of all,

Remind them

You are always with them,

You will never leave,

Your door stays open.

Gracious Father,

We need you.

We love you.

Let us spread your love to others.

Let your will be done.

In Jesus's name,

Amen.